THE HELP YOURSELF
TO ENGLISH
SERIES

THE
RULES
OF
ENGLISH

Edward Marsh

ORIFLAMME PUBLISHING
London

THE RULES OF ENGLISH
in the
HELP YOURSELF TO ENGLISH
series
by Edward Marsh

© Oriflamme Publishing Ltd 1995

ISBN 0 948093 15 3

First Edition 1995

Oriflamme Publishing Ltd.
60 Charteris Road
London N4 3AB

Phototypeset in 12 on 13 point Times New Roman and
Printed and bound in the British Isles by
The Guernsey Press Co. Ltd., Guernsey, Channel Islands.

THE RULES OF ENGLISH
How to use this book

The Rules of English sets out the main principles of correct English usage in the form of two hundred separate rules. Each rule has a title which states approximately the area it deals with. Some rules are simple statements of a particular principle of grammar or sentence construction; others are general statements concerning the usage of particular words or phrases.
The usage in this book is that normally employed in the British Isles.

Spaced out through the book are a series of practice pages, each dealing with one group of rules already covered, and these are listed on the contents page. At the beginning there is a complete list of the rules in the contents pages. At the end of the book there is an index of the main topics referred to in the titles of the rules.

The Rules of English can be used in four ways:

(1) As a textbook

By starting with Rule 1 and working through to Rule 200, doing the exercises on the way, *The Rules of English* can be used as a basic textbook of English grammar and usage.

The rules have been deliberately organized so that the book can be used in just this way. So the early rules deal with some basic definitions that will be needed before any further progress is made. Then follow groups of rules on each of the parts of speech (nouns, verbs, adjectives etc.), in each case starting with basic points, and then moving on to more detailed information. After these sections comes a group of rules on the use of phrases and clauses in sentence construction, and information on the rules of punctuation.

Many children using the book should have have covered some at least of the ground in their junior schools, but probably not in a systematic manner as presented here. Where the book is used in schools it should be introduced to children around the age of nine or ten, and can be used at almost any stage from there upwards, depending on the ability of the pupils concerned. For home use, as a reinforcement or back-up to lessons in school, it is sensible to treat the book as a basic textbook, and work steadily through. Children will more readily grasp some rules than they will others. Some rules will already have been covered in school, others will not. Each individual child will need to work through the topics covered at his own pace, but as a general guide there is nothing here which should be beyond a bright eleven-year-old, or an average thirteen-year-old.

(2) As a revision course

It is also possible to use **The Rules of English** as a revision text for older pupils, such as those studying for school leaving examinations. Where such children have not been taught English grammar and usage in a systematic way at school, they may well need a formal and structured approach at that stage to ensure that they can use the language competently and correctly. For such students, the book is best used as a course of study over a year, or as a crash course over a few months. The same suggestions would equally apply to adults entering for similar examinations which require a good command of basic English.

(3) As a reference book

The provision of an index (at the back of the book) and a full list of the rules by their titles makes it possible to use **The Rules of English** as a convenient reference book to check points of grammar and usage that are not fully understood, or need revision for a specific purpose. The index references should always be checked in the order they are given, since basic information will be contained in the first rule mentioned, with additional information in subsequent rules. The student can then study the rules needed to answer the particular difficulty.

(4) As a study book for those whose first language is not English

For students whose first language is not English, but who have already learnt to read English adequately, **The Rules of English** provides an ideal course in the structure of the language and the way it is used. It is simple, readable, and easy to understand, and the information is broken down into digestible pieces. It provides a fully structured and detailed course, as well as a handy work of reference.

THE SERIES

For those who have found *The Rules of English* helpful, there are five other books in the *Help Yourself to English* series, which will also be of use. They deal with specific topics in the language, and provide additional help and information on the topics covered here. These books are also workbooks as well as textbooks. Each is organized with the text as an information page facing a page of exercises, designed to offer the essential practice.

Book One - Words: basic English grammar
Book Two - Sentences: more advanced grammar and syntax
Book Three - Composition: the techniques of essay writing
Book Four - Comprehension: the techniques of comprehension exercises
Book Five - Spelling: the rules of phonetic spelling
The books are suitable for children aged from eight or nine upwards, and for adult use.
Answer Booklets are also available for all the books in the series, and the present title.

The Rules of English
Contents

Rule 1   Always write in sentences

A sentence is a group of words (or sometimes just one word) that makes sense by itself.

The book is on is not a sentence.
The book is on the table is a sentence.

Where is is not a sentence.
Where is the book ? is a sentence.

Sentences can be statements of fact (like: *The book is on the table.*).

They can be questions (like: *Where is the book ?*).

They can also be commands:
Stop it at once! is a sentence; so is *Stop!*

Most sentences have a **verb**, or **doing word**, which tells you what the action is.

Is is a verb; so is *stop*; so are all these: *writes, sing, has seen, is going, could be, will have waited, had decided, can do, are listening, flew, chased, might want, may come, shall have been chosen.*

Check your own writing to make sure your sentences do have a verb.
You still need to be careful. Some groups of words do have a verb, but are not sentences.

The man that I saw has a verb (*saw*), but it is not a sentence.
It is not a sentence because it does not make sense by itself.
The man that I saw had a black bushy beard is a sentence, because it makes sense.

Rule 2   A sentence must start with a capital letter and end with a full stop.

This is a very simple rule to remember, and easy to get right every time.
It will also remind you to check that each sentence you have written really is a sentence.

The full stop at the end may be a simple full stop, a question mark (?) or an exclamation mark (!).

Rule 3   Every word in English is a part of speech

Part of speech is what we call the job a word does when it used in writing or in speaking.
To understand how English works you need to know what the different parts of speech are, and to recognise what part of speech a word is when it is used. The parts of speech are:
nouns verbs adjectives adverbs pronouns conjunctions prepositions interjections
The following rules tell you what each part of speech is.

Rule 4 Nouns are naming words

Nouns are the words for: **people, places, things, animals, objects**.
They can be special names for single things, people etc., or general names for things.
Boy, woman, house, banana, dog, laughter, sadness, Dr Johnson, New York are all nouns

Rule 5 Verbs are doing words

Verbs tell you what action is happening.
Verbs come in many different forms, depending on the time the action happens, who is doing it, how it is done and so on. A single verb can be made up of several different words, as you will see from the list below.
Verbs are not the names of actions, but the actions themselves. (So *move* is a verb, but *movement* is a noun.)
Goes, come, write, has sung, shall have spoken, can do, is being punished are all verbs.

There is another important verb, which is **not an action**:
the verb **to be**, with its various parts - *is, are, was, were* etc.

Rule 6 Adjectives are describing words

They tell you more about nouns, giving details of what the thing or person is like.
Good, several, new, impossible, three, all, happy, late, huge are all adjectives.

Rule 7 Adverbs describe verbs

They are rather like adjectives, but are used to tell you the way actions are done.
(Adverbs can also be used to describe adjectives, as you will see in a later rule.)
Slowly, quickly, amazingly, really, often, where are all adverbs.

Rule 8 Pronouns are words that act in place of nouns

We use them as a short way of naming people or things, especially when they are performing the action of a verb.
He, she, it, we, us, them, you, who are all pronouns.

Rule 9 Conjunctions are joining words

They link two or more words together, or they may link groups of words together.
And, but, so, or, if are all conjunctions.

Rule 10   Prepositions are placing words

Prepositions go in front of nouns etc. to tell you where or when something is to be found.
On, in, onto, into, over, after, by, of are all prepositions.

Rule 11 Interjections are words that are shouted or exclaimed

Oh! Ow! Ouch! are interjections.
Interjections may be made up of more than one word: *Oh dear!*
Interjections are nearly always followed by an exclamation mark.

Rule 12   There are three articles

These are not really parts of speech (as they should strictly be classed as a special type of adjective). There are only three of them: **the, a, an**; and in fact **an** is only a special form of **a.**

They are placed in front of nouns to show whether the noun concerned is a particular example or a general example of that kind of thing. Very often you will find one or more adjectives between the article and the following noun.
Some rules about the correct use of the articles follow later on.

Rule 13   There are several kinds of nouns

The most common kind of noun is the *common noun.* **Common nouns** are the names of ordinary things, objects, animals etc. They are not special names for one individual thing or person.
Chair, boat, fish, dog, window, man, island, moon, mother, water are common nouns.

Similar are *abstract nouns.* **Abstract nouns** are the names of things like thoughts, feelings etc. which we cannot see, hear, smell, taste or touch.
The *names* of actions are also abstract nouns: so *think* is a verb, but a *thought* is an abstract noun.
Happiness, enjoyment, love, peace, beauty, thought, work, fear, decision, choice are abstract nouns.

The third type of noun is the *collective.* **Collective nouns** are the words used to name a group or collection of people or objects or animals.
Herd, congregation, shoal, swarm, bunch are collective nouns.
There are some important special rules about collective nouns which we shall come to later.

Finally there are *proper nouns.* **Proper nouns** are the special names of individual places, people or things.
Jenny Jones, Fido, Dr Jekyl, Mount Vesuvius, the Atlantic Ocean, Flying Scotsman are proper nouns.
Rule 15 is about the correct use of capital letters for proper nouns.

Rule 14   Some nouns are made up of more than one word

This is clearly true of proper nouns, since some names have more than one word in them. Obviously the two words *New York* are both needed to name that particular city. It would be very silly to call it *New*, and very confusing to call it *York*.

When common nouns are formed with more than one word, the words are quite often linked by **hyphens**. A *hyphen* is a small dash.
Here are some examples: *brother-in-law, by-pass, passer-by, vice-admiral, lady-in-waiting, conveyor-belt.*

On the other hand, in some cases where you might expect a hyphen, it is missing:
chest of drawers, right angle.

When similar groups of words are proper nouns (especially titles) they are less likely to have hyphens:
Master of the Rolls, Lord Chief Justice etc.

When two words have been linked together for a very long time they are generally written as one word:
armchair, bedroom, bookcase, fireman, stepson.
These words are formed from two nouns , the first of which is acting as a permanent adjective.
Rule 40 tells you more about this.

Rule 15   Proper nouns must have capital letters

Proper nouns are names, not just naming words. They can be the names of people, animals, places, things, objects, organizations, almost anything in fact. They are not the general words for any of these though. Each proper noun is the particular name for one particular person, place, thing etc.

You have been told in *Rule 14* that proper nouns may contain more than one word - because of course names sometimes contain more than one word.

All the words that make up a **proper noun** should have a **capital letter** *except* prepositions, conjunctions and articles in the middle of the name. Sometimes when *the* comes in front of a name it may have a capital letter, but only when it is a genuine part of the name. Usually it does not have a capital.

Here are some examples of proper nouns for names of persons - with their capital letters:
Christopher, Alison Warner, Mrs Slade, Father Robin, Sir Derek Sawyer, the Queen of England, Saint Francis of Assisi, the Prophet Mohammed, the Lord Krishna, Jesus Christ.

Notice that when people have a *title*, or just a form of address, that is counted as part of the proper noun, and must also have a capital letter.

Names for places must have capital letters:
Islington, Charteris Road, New Delhi, the United States of America, the British Isles, the Atlantic Ocean, Stow-on-the-Wold, Ashby de la Zouche, Warwick Castle, Saint Mark's Square.

Rule 15 cont.

In fact all names must have capital letters:
Fido (dog), *Red Rum* (horse), *Lyndhurst School, Calcutta University, Fortnum and Mason* (shop), *British Rail, Wakefield Trinity Rugby Football Club, Oriflamme Publishing Limited* (company), *Derbyshire County Council, the Lamb and Flag* (pub), *the Titanic* (ship), *Concorde* (aeroplane), *a Jaguar* (car), *Flying Scotsman* (locomotive), *the Royal Navy, the Foreign Office* (government department), *Alpha Centauri* (star).

Notice that titles of books, films, plays, programmes etc. all need capital letters, and in their case the article (*a, an, the*) often is part of the name, and does need a capital letter:
A Tale of Two Cities (book), *The Nine O'clock News* (programme), *A Midsummer Night's Dream* (play), *The Sound of Music* (film), *The Rime of the Ancient Mariner* (poem).

Rule 16   Some other words must also have capital letters

Titles used by themselves to name a special particular person must also have a capital letter, even when the title can at other times be used as an ordinary common noun:
The Head Master has sent for all the prefects.   Until the Pope's visit, no reigning pope had ever been to England. Long live the Emperor!   The Queen is only the seventh queen to reign in her own right.

Notice when a capital is used and when it is not.

When abstract nouns are used as if they stood for living things they sometimes have a capital letter.
This is known as **personification**: *I love no-one so much as I love Truth.*
In your own writing you can really manage without this, but you may well see it in things you read.

Adjectives formed from proper nouns - from the names of people, places etc. - must have a capital letter:
English, Chinese, Punjabi, Mancunian (meaning 'from Manchester'), *Dickensian* ('like the works of Dickens').
Many of these proper adjectives are often used as nouns: *English* can mean *the English language*; *a Punjabi* is a person from the Punjab.

The **days** of the week and special days have capitals: *Tuesday, Christmas Day, Hallowe'en.*
The **months** also have capitals: *December, June*; but the **seasons do not**: *spring, summer, autumn, winter.*

The pronoun **I** is always a capital letter.
You should already know (*Rule 2*) that sentences must start with a capital letter.

Rule 17   Most nouns form the plural by adding the letter s

Plural simply means *more than one*.
Singular means only *one*.

The vast majority of nouns in English form their plural by adding the letter **s** to the singular.
So: singular - *book*; plural - *books* : singular - *tie*; plural - *ties* : singular - *piece*; plural - *pieces*.

There are, however, exceptions to this rule, and they are listed in *Rules 18 to 31*. It is important that you learn the exceptions, as they are often among the commonest words in the language.

Rule 18   Nouns ending in Y change Y to I and add ES for the plural

This is not particularly complicated. If the singular ends in **y**, the plural ends in **ies**.
So: singular - *story*; plural - *stories* : singular - *cry*; plural - *cries* : singular - *city*; plural - *cities*.

There is an important exception to this rule - set out in *Rule 19*.

Rule 19   Nouns ending in AY, EY, OY and UY simply add S for the plural

This rule concerns the exceptions to *Rule 18*.
In effect, in words ending in **vowel plus y** (*ay, ey, oy, uy*), the plural is formed by adding **s**. The **y** is **not changed**.
So: singular - *way*; plural - *ways* : singular - *key*; plural - *keys* : singular - *boy*; plural - *boys* .

Rule 20   Nouns ending in X, S, SS, SH and CH add ES for the plural

The spelling **es** for the plural of these words is not a problem, as it follows the way we say the words.
So: singular - *fox*; plural - *foxes* : singular - *gas*; plural - *gases* (not 'gasses') : singular - *class*; plural - *classes* :
singular - *wish*; plural - *wishes* : singular - *arch*; plural - *arches*.

Rule 21   Some nouns ending in F change F to V and add ES for the plural

This is a problem rule, because some nouns make the change and some do not. Those that do not simply add an s.
When a noun does make this change, all you have to remember is: ***singular* f, *plural* ves**.

Here are some nouns (showing singular and plural) that do change **f to v** and **add es**:
loaf - loaves; wolf - wolves; shelf - shelves; thief - thieves; leaf - leaves; half - halves;
calf - calves; sheaf - sheaves; self - selves.
The plural pronoun *themselves* (plural of *himself/herself/itself*) is another example.

Some nouns ending in **f** can form their plural either with **ves** *or* just with **s**:
dwarf - dwarves/dwarfs;   elf - elves/elfs;   hoof - hoofs/hooves;   scarf - scarves/scarfs; turf - turfs/turves

Three nouns ending in **fe** also change the **f to v** and add s for the plural:
knife - knives; wife - wives; life - lives.

Apart from the nouns mentioned in the lists above you are unlikely to find many that make the change to *ves*.
The rest just add **s**:
roofs, chiefs, beliefs, cuffs, oafs, reefs, proofs, serfs, cliffs, safes.

Do not make the mistake of applying this rule to nouns which end in **ve** for their singular.
Their plurals will of course be in **ves**:
waves, sleeves, natives, loves, grooves.

Rule 22   Nouns ending in O form the plural by adding S or ES

Many of the nouns ending in **o** are not in everyday use. Here are some of the more common ones.

Nouns ending in **o** with plurals ending in **es**:
echo - echoes, cargo - cargoes, zero - zeroes, hero - heroes, potato - potatoes, tomato - tomatoes, tornado - tornadoes, torpedo - torpedoes, innuendo - innuendoes.
Notice also: *goes* (*How many goes can I have ?*) ; and *noes* (*There were more noes than yeses.*).

Nouns ending in **o** with plural ending in **s**:
banjo - banjos, photo - photos, solo - solos, soprano - sopranos, piano - pianos, halo - halos, falsetto - falsettos, tango - tangos, dynamo - dynamos, fiasco - fiascos, casino - casinos, ghetto - ghettos, piccolo - piccolos.

Abbreviated words like *kilo, disco* and *memo* also usually just add **s** for the plural.
Notice also: *twos* (*Two twos are four.*).

Nouns ending in **o** with plural ending in *either* **s** or **es**:
grotto - grottos/grottoes, domino - dominos/dominoes, stiletto - stilettos/stilettoes, volcano - volcanos/volcanoes, commando - commandos/commandoes, manifesto - manifestos/manifestoes.

The plural ending in **es** is possibly more common than that in **s**, but you will need to learn each new word's plural as
you come across it. You also need to look at the following rule.

Rule 23   Nouns ending in EO, IO, OO, UO and YO form the plural with S

This is the only invariable rule about words ending in **o**. However, it does cover many of these words.
Some examples follow:
folios, radios, cameos, oratorios, ratios, studios, stereos, videos, curios, portfolios, duos, embryos cuckoos, bamboos, cockatoos, kangaroos, tattoos, taboos, shampoos, boos.

Rule 24   Some nouns have the old English plural ending in EN

The only ones you need to know are:
child - children, man - men, woman - women, ox - oxen.

Rule 25   Some nouns change their form in the plural

There are not many nouns that change their form in the plural.
The ones you need to know are:
goose - geese, foot - feet, tooth - teeth, mouse - mice, louse - lice.

Rule 26 Foreign words used in English sometimes keep a foreign plural

Some of the most common examples of these words are listed below.

Words from Latin ending in **us** may form their plurals in **i** :
nucleus - nuclei, gladiolus - gladioli, fungus - fungi, radius - radii, terminus - termini, syllabus - syllabi
Be very careful with the **i** ending. Many words ending in **us** have now become normal English and form their plurals by adding **es**. Even from the examples above *radiuses, syllabuses,* and *terminuses* are now in common use.
Octopuses, hippopotamuses (both from Greek not Latin) and *buses* are correct: plurals in **i** would be wrong.
If in doubt, just use the form ending in **es**.

Words from Latin ending in **um** may form their plurals in **a**:
millennium - millennia, gymnasium - gymnasia, memorandum - memoranda.
The same warning as above applies. The ordinary **s** ending is common for most if not all of such words.

Words from Latin ending in **a** may form their plurals in **ae**:
Formula - plural *formulae* - is the only one in common use; and *formulas* is now more general.

Words from Greek ending in **is** change **is** to **es** for the plural:
crisis - crises, thesis - theses, analysis - analyses, synthesis - syntheses, paralysis - paralyses, diagnosis - diagnoses, metamorphosis - metamorphoses. Notice the confusing plural of *axis: axes.*

Words from Greek ending in **on** form their plurals in **a** :
automaton - automata, criterion - criteria, phenomenon - phenomena.
Be careful once again. There are many words ending in **on** (whether or not they come from Greek) which can only form their plural with an **s**: *horizons, prisons, reasons, lemons, millions, billions* etc.

Words from French ending in **eau** add **x** for the plural:
chateau - chateaux, gateau - gateaux, bureau - bureaux, portmanteau - portmanteaux.
All the above may also add **s**; and in the case of *plateau,* both *plateaux* and *plateaus* are equally common.

Two other foreign plurals you may come across are: *cherub - cherubim, seraph - seraphim* (both from Hebrew).

Rule 27 Nouns made up of several words make the main word plural

So: *mother in law/mothers in law; by-pass/by-passes; passer-by/passers-by; man-of-war* (meaning a battleship or a jellyfish)/***men-of-war;*** *commander-in-chief/commanders-in-chief; court-martial/courts martial.*
The only notable exception seems to be: *sergeant-major/sergeant-majors.*

Rule 28 Figures and letters use an apostrophe to form the plural

So: *1's, 2's, 3's, 10's, a's, b's, c's, p's and q's.*
Do **not** use the apostrophe with any **other plurals**.

Rule 29   Proper nouns nearly always form the plural with S or ES

So: *Mr Smith - the Smiths; the two Christophers* etc.

If the proper noun ends in **s**, the plural will add **es**: *Mrs Lewis - the Lewises.*
However, if this produces a clumsy result, it is possible simply to leave the noun unchanged:
Mr Sanders - the Sanders. (A better way to deal with this would be to write: *the Sanders family.*)

If the proper name ends in **y**, **add s** for the plural; **do not** change the *y* to *i* and add *es* :
the two Lucys; Miss Terry - the Terrys etc.

Rule 30   Some nouns do not change in the plural

So: *deer, sheep, salmon, cannon, corps, cod, grouse, trout, series, species.*
The most common words covered by this rule are names of certain animals and (especially) fish,
and a few words that end in **s** for their singular.

Rule 31   Some nouns have two plural forms which may have different meanings

So: *penny - pence, pennies : fish - fish, fishes*
index - indexes, indices (used for the little figures written after numbers to mean squared etc.)
shot - shot (pieces of shot; cannonballs etc.), *shots* (bullets fired)
glass - glass (sheets of glass), *glasses* (several drinking glasses, or a pair of spectacles)
cloth - cloths (pieces of cloth), *clothes* (which people wear)
medium - mediums (averages or psychics !). *The media* means newspapers, radio and television taken as a whole;
and is still plural, though often treated as singular.

Rule 32   Some nouns have no singular

So: *trousers, shorts, scissors, shears, pliers, spectacles* (rather like *glasses* mentioned in *Rule 31*), *thanks, cattle.*

Anything which comes joined in two sections is usually a plural noun. We often put the words *a pair of* in front of
this sort of plural noun: *a pair of shorts, a pair of spectacles, a pair of scissors* etc.
We can also say *a pair of socks* etc. (even though *socks* does have a singular - *sock*).

The word *news* started its existence as plural (meaning *new things*), but is now singular.

The words *data* (meaning information or facts) and *strata* (meaning layers - usually of rock) both started life as
plurals, and had singular forms (*datum, stratum*), but they are now often treated as if they were singular.

Rule 33   Some nouns are singular by nature

There are some things which really **cannot be counted**, and so the nouns that stand for them do not have plurals, or have plurals which are only used in special cases. These nouns fall into three main groups:

(1) Many **abstract** nouns:
biology, geography, education, information, homework, knowledge, wisdom, advice, evidence, help, assistance, patience, progress, advancement, music, love, enjoyment - and many others.

Even words of this sort have plurals when used in different ways: *I have read two histories of this period* is quite correct because, though *history* cannot be counted, it is used here to mean *history book*.

(2) **Food** and **drink** (and other **liquids**):
water, tea, coffee, soup, beer, milk, oil, petrol; butter, margarine, flour, sugar, salt, pepper, rice, pasta, honey, bread, meat, pork, beef, etc.

Once again we can still ask for: *Two teas, and two coffees, each with two sugars* - because we mean something rather different: *cups of tea and coffee, spoonfuls of sugar.*
Though *cheese* is an uncountable noun of this sort we can still talk about *cheeses*, often meaning *types of cheese*, and we can certainly use *waters* meaning *seas* or *rivers*.

(3) **Materials** and **substances**: *gold, brass, cotton, silk, wood, paper* and *glass* (which has already been mentioned in *Rule 31* - where both its separate plural forms have special meanings).

The special plural uses exist here too: *silks and satins* means *clothes made of silk and satin*; *the papers* means *the newspapers*, and *papers* means *documents*; *brasses* means *brass ornaments*; *woods* means *forests*.

There are a few **other** naturally singular nouns, without common plural forms. You should note:
accommodation, furniture, luggage, baggage, rubbish, equipment, cash, weather, mankind.

We talk about all these sorts of items by using words that mean a **part**, or a **quantity** of the item:
a piece of cheese, a slice of bread, a portion of jam, a pinch of salt, a cup of tea, a glass of water, a can of petrol, an item of luggage, a bit of advice, a moment of time.
We also often use words like **some** and **any** with them: *Do you want any sugar ? No, but I'd like some honey.*

Rule 34   Some groups have a special collective noun

It is always possible to use a general collective noun like *group* or *collection*, *crowd* or *set*, but there are some particular ones. Here are a few of the more common ones you may meet:

People: *band/orchestra of musicians, board of directors, choir of singers, class of pupils, company of actors, crew of sailors, gang/den of thieves, staff of teachers/employees, team of players*

Animals: *flock of birds/sheep, herd of cattle/deer/horses, litter of young (animals), shoal/school of fish, pack of wolves/dogs, plague of locusts, swarm of insects*

Things: *bunch of flowers, fleet of ships, pack of cards, clump of trees, peal of bells.*
There are very many more. Try to remember them as you come across them.

Rule 35 Nouns have a possessive formed with the apostrophe and S

The possessive (in grammar) means **belonging to**. We can also show it by using the conjunction **of**:
the book of the boy   -   the pen of the girl   -   the kennel of the dog.
The order is always: ***object owned - of - owner.***

The possessive form is a shorter way of writing the same thing.
It is formed by adding **apostrophe s** to the noun.
An apostrophe is a single mark like a **comma**, written **above the line**.

Here are the three examples given above written using the possessive:
the boy's book - the girl's pen - the dog's kennel
This is the way of forming all possessives for words in the **singular** - including words ending in *s* or *y*:
the church's spire, the lady's hat, the gas's volume, the people's choice, the monkey's tricks.

As you know most nouns in English form their **plural** by adding **s**.
When we want to use the **possessive** of a **plural noun** we do it rather differently.
Plural nouns ending in **s** form their possessive by adding an **apostrophe after the s**.
They do **not** add **another s**.

So if the examples were:
the books of the boys   -   the pens of the girls   - the kennels of the dogs;
their possessive forms would be:
the boys' books   -   the girls' pens   -   the dogs' kennels.
Here are some other examples:
the churches' spires, the babies' toys, the princesses' gowns, the horses' oats.

For **plural** nouns that do **not** end in **s**, the possessive is formed by adding **apostrophe s**.
So these words are treated as if they were singular:
the men's hats, the children's games, the geese's eggs, the mice's holes, the genii's bottles.

For **proper nouns**, the possessive is formed in the same way as for other nouns:
John's bike, Mr Chamberlain's umbrella, The Titanic's funnels, Derby County's team.
Notice that when the proper noun has **several words** in it, the **apostrophe s** goes on the **last word** :
the Lord Chief Justice's book.
Proper nouns ending in s may form their possessive by adding either **apostrophe s**, or just an **apostrophe**:
James' book/ James's book, Mrs Sanders' book, the Jacksons' (plural) books.
Notice: *the Joneses' book* where the proper noun has a plural in *es,* to which the apostrophe is then added.

Look at these tables of the different sorts of possible possessives:

one book of one boy	*the boy's book*	*one hat of one woman*	*the woman's hat*
one book of several boys	*the boys' book*	*one hat of several women*	*the women's hat*
several books of one boy	*the boy's books*	*several hats of one woman*	*the woman's hats*
several books of several boys	*the boys' books*	*several hats of several women*	*the women's hats*

Remember these hints:
Do not use apostrophes to form the plural, only to form the possessive. (But see *Rule28.*)
Make sure you put the apostrophe on the owner, not the thing owned.
Do not change the word to make the possessive, just add *apostrophe s*, or an *apostrophe alone* for plurals in *s*.

Rule 36   With some nouns use the possessive, with others use OF

With **people**, **animals**, and many **proper nouns** generally, the possessive with **apostrophe s** is usually used.
For example:
John's homework, the girls' room, Spot's kennel, our team's victory (The team is made up of people!),
the pupils' misbehaviour, the children's ward, the nation's triumph, the king's coronation,
Mallard's record (*Mallard* is a locomotive), *'Ivanhoe's' opening chapter* ('*Ivanhoe*' is a book).
Even with some of the above **of** could be used: *the misbehaviour of the pupils,* for example.
Notice the possessive in phrases like: *at the greengrocer's* - which is really a short way of saying
at the greengrocer's shop.

With **longer names** (even names of just two words) it is better to use **of**.
For example: *The first verse of 'The Lady of Shalott'* ('*The Lady of Shalott*' is a poem).

Places can use **either**:
England's glory, Germany's defeat, the sights of Calcutta, the site of the Black Hole.
Notice that *the ruins of Rievaulx Abbey* is better than *Rievaulx Abbey's ruins* because of the two-word name.

Maps always have **of** followed by the place name: *a street-map of Bremerhaven.*

If in doubt with **names**, use **of**, rather than the apostrophe.

It is much less usual to use the possessive with an apostrophe for common nouns, but not wrong to do so.
The door of the house, the remains of the feast, the end of the road, the still of the night are the strictly correct
forms, but: *the church's spire, the breakers' roar, the bicycle's wheel, the traffic's noise, a century's neglect*
are all now good English.
For **common nouns**, if in doubt, use **of**.

Nouns used for measurements or periods **of time** use the **apostrophe s** form, not the *of* form:
yesterday's news, a moment's pleasure, two years' imprisonment.

It is quite possible to have **two possessives** linked to **one noun** (*the new secretary's boss's house*), but it is better to
change one of them to the form with *of*, even if speaking about a person (*the house of the new secretary's boss*).
When there are **two** forms with **of** following each other, it is common to change one of them to the possessive,
even if it is a word where the *of* form is more usual:
The sound of the clock's ticking and *the sound of the ticking of the clock* are both, however, correct.

One final curious usage you should notice is when **of and the apostrophe** are used **together**, when talking about
one example of several, without any extra detail. This is only used when talking about a particular person.
Another way of saying the same thing is to use **one of**.

These examples show both forms:
a friend of Robert's (one of Robert's friends), a tape of my sister's (one of my sister's tapes).

In the following the double possessive would not be right, as a specific person is not involved:
a decision of the board (**not** *board's*), *the votes of the people* (**not** *people's*).
In *a friend of the family* (**rather than** *family's*), it is borderline; the double possessive might be used.
If in doubt about a double possessive, however, it is safest not to use it.

PRACTICE ONE

Exercise 1

Write out each of the following groups of words, and next to it write **sentence** or **not sentence**.
If you think it is a sentence, write it starting with a capital letter and ending with a full stop
(or question mark or exclamation mark).
(1) a long road   (2) come here, Sally   (3) I do not think so   (4) meet me after school
(5) where are you (6) after the people had all been evacuated from the burning building
(7) please tell me where Elizabeth has gone (8) where has Elizabeth gone
(9) please tell me (10) we can see you   (11) the lady who was waiting for the number seven bus
(12) where it was   (13) she didn't, did she   (14) beginning to rain   (15) then it happened
(16) when you are feeling better   (17) even though it will take a very long time
(18) my two sisters, Amanda from next door and her mother, Mrs Ponsonby, and the vicar of course
(19) can Jimmy come out to play this afternoon, please, Mrs Wilson   (20) no, he can't

Exercise 2

Write down each of the following words, and next to each word write what part of speech it is.
If it can be more than one part of speech write both down.
(1) boy   (2) write   (3) funny   (4) slowly   (5) but
(6) the   (7) of   (8) Ouch !   (9) he   (10) new
(11) knew   (12) choose   (13) soon   (14) cupboard   (15) herself
(16) clever   (17) at   (18) animal   (19) think   (20) red

Exercise 3

(a) Each of the following words can be more than one part of speech. For each word write the different parts
of speech it could be. The number of possible parts of speech is shown after the word.
(1) place (two)   (2) fly (two)   (3) wrong (three)   (4) fast (three)

(b) When you have got the right answer to the first part of the exercise, go on to use these words in ten different
sentences of your own, one sentence for each part of speech. After each sentence write the word, and the part
of speech it is in that sentence.

Exercise 4

Say what part of speech the words underlined in each sentence are:
(1) What do you want for Christmas, little girl ? (2) He told me to wait for you here.
(3) After a good race, he was the clear winner.   (4) We looked at him in amazement.
(5) I remember where she went last time.   (6) Suddenly we saw it running swiftly towards us.
(7) This is a page from the book.   (8) He has told me what he was doing there.
(9) Is it necessary to start a new page ?   (10) The armed forces of the allies are now in action.

Exercise 5

The following words are all nouns. Say whether each one is common, collective, proper, or abstract.
(1) book   (2) science   (3) herd   (4) sight   (5) Mr John Smith
(6) reason   (7) water   (8) crowd   (9) computer (10) congregation
(11) Goliath   (12) flock   (13) socks   (14) queen   (15) New Street Station
(16) age   (17) hope   (18) rice   (19) action   (20) emperor

Exercise 6

Write out these sentences, giving capital letters to those words which should have them.
(1) The queen has asked the president of the united states to meet her at windsor castle.
(2) For this course we have to read great expectations by charles dickens, and tolstoy's war and peace.
(3) Unless an englishman has actually lived in china, he will have have great difficulty learning chinese.
(4) "The lady and i are just good friends," claimed the bishop of bognor in an interview in the moon newspaper.

Exercise 7

Give the plural of these nouns:
(1) house   (2) cloud   (3) shoe   (4) letter   (5) song   (6) fly   (7) supply
(8) lie   (9) lily   (10) salary   (11) holiday   (12) survey   (13) buoy   (14) monkey
(15) scarf   (16) church   (17) mass   (18) gas   (19) lock   (20) box   (21) dish
(22) cliff   (23) wolf   (24) shelf   (25) leaf   (26) knife   (27) proof   (28) soliloquy
(29) elf (two answers).

Exercise 8

Give the plural of these nouns
(1) tornado   (2) solo   (3) piano   (4) volcano (two answers)   (5) folio   (6) cameo
(7) embryo   (8) innuendo   (9) kangaroo   (10) duo   (11) child   (12) ox   (13) goose
(14) mouse   (15) gateau   (16) moron   (17) crisis   (18) labyrinth   (19) sheep   (20) James
(21) genius (two answers)   (22) lady-in-waiting   (23) 7   (24) phenomenon
(25) man-of-war   (26) lord chief justice   (27) scissors   (28) rice

Exercise 9

Give the singular of these nouns
(1) daisies   (2) teeth   (3) monkeys   (4) choices   (5) wives
(6) trout   (7) trousers   (8) milk   (9) automata   (10) potatoes

Exercise 10

Give the two possessive forms, singular then plural, (with an apostrophe) of each of the following words:
(1) girl   (2) man   (3) fox   (4) baby   (5) wife
(6) church   (7) donkey   (8) dove   (9) lady-in-waiting   (10) impresario

Exercise 11

Change from singular into plural (both nouns must be changed):
(1) the boy's bike   (2) the house's chimney   (3) the lord chief justice's wig
(4) the abbey's ruin   (5) the woman's child

Change from plural into singular (both nouns):
(6) the choirs' performances (7) the termini's facilities   (8) the schoolmistresses' spectacles
(9) the geese's goslings   (10) the by-laws' complexities

Exercise 12

Give the special collective nouns for a group of each of the following:
(1) cattle   (2) sheep   (3) puppies   (4) lions   (5) pigeons
(6) governors (7) thieves   (8) books   (9) stars (two answers)

Rule 37 There are several types of adjective

You should remember that adjectives are describing words. They add to the meaning of the noun.
The commonest sort of adjective is the adjective of quality, but there are also several others which
you should recognise.

Adjectives of **quality** tell you **what kind** of thing the noun is:
beautiful, grey, foolish, heavy, serious, important, excellent, ambitious, miserable, grateful, huge, sharp, trivial.

Adjectives of **quantity** tell you **how much** or **how many** of the noun is or are there.
They may be *definite*: *one, ten, twenty, hundreds, seven hundred, first, second, third, fortieth, double, treble.*
They may be *indefinite* (vague): *many, some, several, few, much, more, most.*

Adjectives of **distinction** answer the questions **which, what** or **whose** about their noun.
They may be *demonstrative* (pointing out): *this, that, these, those.*
They may be *possessive*: *my, your, his, her, our, their.*
They may be *interrogative* (asking questions): *which, what, whose.*

You do not need to learn these names, but you do need to know when words are being used as adjectives. The main
thing to remember is that an adjective normally goes with (or is linked to) a noun.
Many of the words in the last group of adjectives mentioned here can also in fact be pronouns. They are adjectives
when they are with a noun, as in the following examples:
Those girls are responsible. This book is very useful. Is he your brother?
Which ice-cream do you want ? What mark did you get ? Whose house is it ? It's their house.

Rule 38 Adjectives go before the noun they describe

The correct position for an **adjective** is **in front** of its noun: *a sad day, the silly boy, glorious weather, hard luck.*
If you use **two adjectives** in front of a noun you may link them with a **conjunction**. This is usually *and*, but
sometimes can be others, such as *but* and *or*:
the long and weary journey, a high and mighty prince, a sad but true comment.
We tend only to put in a conjunction if we want to *stress* one or both of the adjectives.
It is more usual simply to separate **two adjectives** used in this way with a **comma**:
the ancient, ruined castle; a distant, eerie cry; weird, shapeless forms.
In modern English, it is now normal not even to put the comma in, especially with common, everyday adjectives:
a silly little boy, the big red car, long blond hair, nice new dresses.
With **three or more adjectives** in front of a noun, it is usual to separate the **first two** (or more) with a **comma**,
and to put the conjunction **and** before the **final** adjective. Do not put a comma in front of the *and*.
So: *an unhappy, disagreeable and pointless occasion; a beautiful, faultless and professional performance,*
a swift, sleek and silent car.
Even so, it is still quite common to use three adjectives separated only by commas, or even not separated at all:
a final, quiet, friendly word; a sudden, momentary, vivid flash;
a bright, cheerful young girl; the old tattered brown hat.

Notice that adjectives of **number** (the numbers themselves, and words like *some* and *any*) do not seem to count as
adjectives for the purpose of commas: they go first, and the next adjective follows directly:
the first grim, grey, shadowy form; three large, red, juicy apples; several suspicious and undesirable characters.

Rule 39   There is a correct order for adjectives in front of nouns

If you look at these words: *a big red British bus*; and compare them with: *a British red big bus*; you will see what this rule is about. The correct order for different types of adjectives is as follows:

(1) Adjectives which give the number: *five, some, any, several*
(2) Adjectives which give an opinion: *good, glorious, bad, unwelcome*
(3) Adjectives which tell you about size: *tiny, small, large, gigantic*
(4) Adjectives which tell you about age: *ancient, old, new, modern*
(5) Adjectives which tell you about colour: *red, white, blue*
(6) Adjectives which tell you what place: *English, foreign*
(7) Adjectives which tell you what kind: *wooden, rural, scientific*

You are very unlikely to find more than three or four adjectives from the above list together of course,
and should not, in your own writing, use long lists of adjectives.
The only doubtful words will be general descriptions, which may be either an opinion about the noun being
described (second position), or a definition of the kind of thing (position seven). Try saying aloud what you want
to
write with the adjective in each place, and choose the one that sounds best.

Here are some examples, with the type of adjective indicated by number as in the list above:
some (1) large (3), white (5), nylon (7) vests;   a huge (3) old (4) iron (7) kettle;
current (4) Japanese (6) technical (7) superiority;   the first (1) glorious (2), English (6) goal;
two (1) small (3) but perfect (2), black and white (5), Etruscan (6) ceramic (7) pots.
Notice in the last example how adjectives that belong together can be linked separately in the list by their own
conjunctions (even if it means breaking the rule about order as in: *small but perfect*).

If you use a different order for adjectives you will stress those particular adjectives. In the first example above,
if you wrote: *a British big red bus*, you would be stressing the fact that it was British.

Rule 40   Nouns may be used as adjectives

Nouns used in this way are generally of the type mentioned under *category 7* in the rule before: they tell you
what kind of thing is being described. They should go next to the noun, after any other adjectives being used.
bus ticket, railway station, stair carpet, cricket match, rice pudding, computer programme, garden shed.

When two nouns are used together in this way very frequently, they may be linked by a hyphen:
lawn-mower, mouse-trap, door-mat, rock-bottom, story-teller, jaw-bone, sea-water, coal-scuttle, dog-biscuit.
These words should be treated as one word, and not separated by an adjective or anything else.

Sometimes two nouns have become completely linked and are written as one word. For example:
moonlight, penknife, hosepipe, fireman, shipwreck, rearguard, clipboard, keynote.
This does happen very often in English, and it is sensible to check in the dictionary to see if a hyphen should or
should not be used, or if the two words must be written as one.
These three examples with *ice-, table-* and *fire-* will show the difficulties involved:
ice hockey, ice-cream, iceberg;   table tennis, table-mat, tablespoon;   fire brigade, fire-escape, fireside.

If for some reason you are not able to check which form is correct, it is acceptable to write most combined or
hyphenated words as two separate words.

Rule 41   Adjectives can be formed from nouns

Many nouns form their own adjectives, generally by adding an ending to the form of the noun. There are very many adjectival endings of this sort, and you will need to learn each one as you come across it. You should also be prepared for other changes in spelling between noun and adjective.

Here are some examples of nouns and the adjectives formed from them:
centre- central, industry - industrial, pole - polar, value - valuable, horror - horrible, type - typical, hero - heroic, fortune - fortunate, noise - noisy, friend - friendly, fool - foolish, beauty - beautiful, mystery - mysterious.

Sometimes more than one adjective can be formed from the same noun, and the resulting adjectives may well have different meanings: *sense - sensible/sensitive.*

Rule 42   Nouns can be formed from adjectives

The reverse process to that described in the rule before is also common. Many adjectives can be used to form a noun (generally an abstract noun) by putting an ending on them.
The most common endings of this sort are **ness** and **ity/ty**, but there are many others.
It is best to check in a dictionary when forming an adjective if you are in doubt.
It is not wise simply to add -*ness*, and hope for the best.
Here are a few of them, showing the adjective followed by the noun formed from it:
like - likeness, silly - silliness, equal - equality, able - ability, cruel - cruelty accurate - accuracy, distant - distance, prudent - prudence, just - justice, wise - wisdom.

Rule 43   Nouns in the possessive may be used together with adjectives

The main point with this rule is to see that the adjective is linked to the correct word.
Look at these examples:
a new boys' bicycle - *a new bicycle designed for use by boys (rather than girls)*
a boy's new bicycle - *a new bicycle belonging to a (particular) boy*
a new-boy's bicycle - *a bicycle belonging to a new boy (new at a particular school)*
(In this last example, the use of the hyphen helps to make the meaning clear.)

In general the rule about order for this sort of phrase is:
(1) adjectives that go with the possessive
(2) the possessive noun
(3) adjectives that go with the main noun
(4) the main noun.

Here are some examples: *the old man's new car, the bad little girl's terrible behaviour, the bird's sweet song.*

When there are two possessives, and several adjectives involved, it is sensible to change one of the possessives to the form that uses **of**:
the former teacher of my old friend's young sister; **not**: *my old friend's young sister's former teacher.*

Rule 44   Adjectives have comparative and superlative forms

The basic form of an adjective is known as its positive form. There are two other forms: the comparative and the superlative. We use these when we are comparing the qualities described; or saying to what extent the adjective applies - whether it is an ordinary amount, or more than usual, or a great deal.
The way this is done with most adjectives is to add **er** for the comparative, and **est** for the superlative:

Positive: *long*	**Comparative**: *longer*	**Superlative**: *longest*
bright	*brighter*	*brightest*
cold	*colder*	*coldest*

So *longer* means *more long* than something (or *more long than usual*);
and *longest* means the *most long* of several examples (or *the most long of all*).

You should use the comparative form when you are making a comparison between only two cases. When you are comparing three or more possible cases, you can use the superlative for one of them:
Sirius is the brightest star. Jackie is the slower of the two girls. What is the shortest route ?
Your car is fast, but mine is faster. Mine is faster than yours. I have the fastest car in London.
The weather is usually fine in France, but it is finer in Spain, and finest in North Africa.
The sun is brighter than the moon. He is older than me but younger than you.

When you are comparing one thing with another you use the **comparative** adjective plus **than**, as you can see in some of the examples above.
Notice that we can use the **comparative** plus **any** (anyone, anything etc.) for a general comparison (even though more than two items are involved):
taller than anyone else in the class, longer than any other opera.

When comparing three or more items, or making a general comparison we use the **superlative** plus **of**.
For example: *Gold is harder than lead, but of lead, gold and iron, iron is the hardest.*

Notice we often use **superlative** plus **of all** for a general comparison: *Steel is the hardest of all.*

Also notice that we very often use **the** in front of a superlative adjective, and quite often in front of a comparative:
*He is **the** best in the world. It was **the** most terrible accident I have ever seen. You are **the** more guilty of the two.*
This makes the superlative specific to the particular example, and emphasizes it.

Sometimes when you are adding a third item to an existing comparison, an extra comparative is included:
John is older than me, but Jack is older than both of us (because *both of us* is treated as one item).
My journey that morning was longer than usual, but my return in the evening was to be longer still.

Notice the use of **comparative** plus **still**. A more common way of doing this is: **even** plus **comparative**. So in this example, we could have written: *even longer* instead of *longer still*.

Finally, there are some adjectives which have no comparative or superlative because of their meaning.
The best known is: *unique* (meaning the only one of its kind). Some other adjectives should also fall into this category, such as *impossible* (because there cannot be degrees of impossibility), but in practice the comparatives and superlatives are used.

Rule 45 The spelling must be changed to form some comparatives and superlatives

There are two main cases where the spelling changes when adding the comparative and superlative endings:

(1) When an adjective ends in a **single cons
onant** following a **short vowel**, such as:
mad, flat, red, thin, slim and *hot*, the **final consonant** is **doubled**.
So the comparatives and superlatives of the examples just mentioned are:
madder/maddest, flatter/flattest, redder/reddest, thinner/thinnest; slimmer/slimmest, hotter/hottest.

(2) When an adjective ends in a **y**, the **y is changed to i,** before adding the ending:
naughty - naughtier - naughtiest; dry - drier - driest; silly - sillier - silliest
Notice the exception: *sly - slyer - slyest.*

Also notice that this rule does **not** apply to adjectives ending in a **vowel plus y** (*ay, ey, oy, uy*):
grey - greyer - greyest.

When the adjective ends in **e**, just **add r or st** for the comparative and superlative:
nice - nicer - nicest.

Rule 46 Longer adjectives use MORE and MOST for comparative and superlative

For the most part, this rule applies to adjectives with **three or more syllables**.
Syllables are the sounds that make up the word. So *horrible* has three syllables: *horr -ib -le*.
Here are some examples of longer adjectives that form their comparative and superlative in this way:
unpleasant - more unpleasant - most unpleasant, **not** *unpleasanter, unpleasantest*
dangerous - more dangerous - most dangerous, **not** *dangerouser, dangerousest*
beautiful - more beautiful - most beautiful, **not** *beautifuler, beautifulest.*

The reason for the different forms of comparative and superlative is that adding the usual endings would make the words very clumsy and difficult to say.
For the same reason there are several **shorter words** (two syllable) which also use **more/most**:
rigid - more rigid - most rigid.
You must choose the form which sounds right and is easiest to say. In some cases, **both** the alternatives are in use:
clever - cleverer/more clever - cleverest/most clever.

Rule 47 Some comparatives and superlatives are irregular

Irregular simply means *not obeying the rule.*
Here are the three adjectives with irregular comparative and superlative forms that you must learn if you do not already know them (but check the next rule as well):

good - better - best   *bad - worse - worst*   *many - more - most.*

Rule 48   Some comparatives and superlatives have two forms

Here are the ones to learn. Notice the different meanings for the different forms:

little - littler - littlest (referring to size)
little - less - least (referring to amount or quantity)

old - older - oldest (in general use)
old - elder - eldest (used for members of a family and other special groups)

late - later - latest (referring to time)
late - latter - last (referring to order or sequence)
The latter means *the second,* or *the one most recently mentioned.*

far - farther - farthest (used for distances)
far - further - furthest (*Further* means *additional; furthest* means the same as *farthest.*)

Less and **least** are often used in effect as opposites of *more* and *most*, when things are being compared for decreasing rather than increasing qualities:
That is the least desirable option.   He is less capable than his brother; his brother is the more intelligent.

Rule 49   The three forms of the article have different uses

The articles are placed in front of nouns to distinguish between their particular and general uses.

The is the **definite article**, and is used for *particular* nouns, singular or plural.
A is the **indefinite article**. It is used for *general* examples of things. It is used only with *singular* nouns.
An is a form of the **indefinite article**. It is used in front of words beginning with a *vowel*.

Words being used in a **general** sense in the **plural** do *not* have an article.

Detailed rules about the use of each of the articles follow.

Rule 50   The definite article is the word: THE

The is known as the definite article because it is used when we mean a **particular** or **definite** thing. It may be used when we will automatically know which particular thing is meant, when the thing is well-known to everyone, or when the thing concerned has already been mentioned. It can be used with singular or plural nouns:
the boys in my class, **the** *house next door,* **the** *tree at* **the** *end of the garden.*

You can see the difference between the general use (*no article*) and the particular use (*the*) in this example:
Boys are always mischievous. **The boys** *in form three are no exception.*

Examples of **the** used with with well-known or immediately recognised words are:
He plays **the** *drums (or any musical instrument).* **The miners** *are on strike.* **The** *government has been defeated.*

Rule 51   The definite article is used with some place names

Most **proper nouns**, including all personal names, do **not** have any article, definite or indefinite.
This rule lists some exceptions, which do have the definite article.

The only **place names** which start with **the** are:

(1) place names which are **plural**   *the United States of America (and the U.S.A.), the British Isles,*
                                         the Himalayas, the Steppes
(2) place names which are **collective** *the Commonwealth, the United Kingdom*
(3) **rivers, seas and oceans**   *the Severn, the River Nile, the Caspian, the North Sea, the Pacific Ocean*
(4) names including a **preposition** *the Isle of Wight, the City of London*
(5) names of **buildings**   *the Great Pyramid, the White House*
(6) names of vague **regions**   *the Midland Plain, the Deccan, the Great Rift Valley*

Do not make the mistake of giving a definite article to: (singular) countries (*England*, **not** *the England*); lakes (notice that we can therefore speak of *the Aral Sea*, but *Lake Aral*); islands (*Easter Island, Fair Isle*); singular mountains (*Mount Everest*, **not** *the Mount Everest*); names of most roads and streets (*Watling Street* and *Station Road*) unless those names are also descriptions: *the Great North Road* and (in India) *the Grand Trunk Road*, for example); names of towns and cities (except **the** *Hague* - capital of **the** Netherlands).

Buildings which start with a personal name (*St.Bartholomew's Hospital, Nelson's Column*) do **not** have an article.

Notice: *the North* etc., *the South Pole, the Equator.*

Be prepared for exceptions; place names are often a matter of usage and choice.

Rule 52   Many proper nouns do not have any article

Personal names do not have an article - but **titles** (when used as a proper noun with a capital letter) do have **the**:
Mr Major (**not** *the Mr Major*), *the Prime Minister, the Pharaoh of Egypt, the Prophet, the Messiah.*

Some very important **books** - in particular the scriptures of various faiths have a definite article:
the Bible (the Holy Bible), the Quran (the Glorious Quran), the Upanishads, the Bhagavadh Gita.

Names of **institutions** formed of **two parts** with a preposition (usually *of*) **do** have the definite article (as with geographical names of this type, mentioned in the rule before):
the Board of Trade, the Commission for Racial Equality, the House of Lords, the Court of Appeal,

Other Institutions, companies and organizations generally do **not** have an article:
Imperial Chemical Industries, Lutterworth Grammar School, Islington Council,
British Rail (but notice: *the Great Central Railway* etc.), *Nottingham Forest Football Club.*

Notable **exceptions**, however, are trade unions and clubs:
the Transport and General Workers Union, the Automobile Association, the Pony Club, the Athenaeum.
Rather similar are: *the Stock Exchange, the Catholic Church, the British Library.*
Because there are many exceptions, you will need to learn them by practice.

Special **events** have a **definite article**: *the Boat Race, the Cup Final, the Fifth Test.*

Rule 53   Many nouns do not normally have any article

You have already seen several examples of proper nouns which do not have an article.
You also know that nouns used generally in the plural do not have an article (as there is no plural of a/an).

It is also unusual for **abstract nouns** to have an article, unless they are used in a particular sense to refer to one specific example - in which case they will need a definite article.
These examples should help you:
He loves music. Age shall not weary them. She is studying biology. I cannot bear pain. Silence is golden.
Hope shall never die. Do you like oriental art ? Stress is bad for you. It causes heart disease.

In the following examples a particular case is meant: ***The** music of Wagner is my favourite.*
***The** life of the king is slipping away. I cannot endure **the** stress of **the** modern age.*

The whole group of nouns which are **singular by nature** - that is, do not have a plural in their normal use -
tends not to use any article. Many of these nouns are mentioned in *Rule 33*, and you should check back to that, but the main things involved are: food and drink, liquids, materials and substances. For example:
It is made of iron. How many yards of cloth do you want ? Don't you like milk ?
These nouns are often found with **some** and **any**:
Do you take sugar ? Have some fruit. I don't want any meat.

When one of these words is used to mean a particular item, however, you do sometimes see them with a definite article, and should use the definite article when you mean a particular example:
*Strike while **the** iron is hot. **The** cloth is very fine. **The** coffee they serve here is awful.*

Rule 54   Adjectives go between article and noun

This is a very straightforward rule. For example:
a fast car, a big red bus, the long, slow hours of night, the recent murder, an empty shelf.

Treat **some** and **any** as if they were articles, and always put them first.

Rule 55   A is used before a consonant, AN is used before a vowel

The vowels are **a, e, i, o, u.** So in front of words beginning with these letters we use **an** as the indefinite article:
an apple, an egg, an igloo, an orange, an umpire, an awful waste, an excellent result, an icy reception.
Notice that it is the word ***immediately*** following the article which determines whether it is *a* or *an*.

There is an **exception** to the above rule involving the **letter u.**
When **u** at the beginning of a word has the same **sound** as the word *you*, then an indefinite article in front of it will be **a** rather than ***an***: *a unicorn, a united front, a useful implement.*

The indefinite article **an** is also used in front of words that begin with a **silent h** (an *h* which is not pronounced):
an heir, an hour, an honourable decision, but: *a horse, a house, a history lesson.*
Both *a hotel* and *an hotel* are correct (but the *h* is now nearly always said, so *a hotel* is more common).

Rule 56   The indefinite article has several uses

The indefinite article is used when we are mentioning something in general, or any one out of many, rather than a particular example. It is also used when we are mentioning something for the first time, and when we are mentioning something about which we have no other information:
*Do you want **an** ice-cream* (any ice-cream, not a particular one) ?   *A man was asking for you* (a man mentioned for the first time). *There is **a** new girl in our class* (but there is no further information about her).

In each of these examples, if the noun introduced by the indefinite article were used again, it would now require a definite article (*the*), because some information at least has been provided in the sentence given, and we are now referring back to a known quantity.

Rule 57   The indefinite article may only be used with singular nouns.

The uses of the indefinite article, mentioned in the rule before, only apply to nouns in the singular.
There is no plural form of the indefinite article, and in the cases described above, **no** article would be used for plural examples.

However, we often find it necessary to use something, rather than just the word by itself.
In these cases **some** is used rather like a plural indefinite article:
There are some new girls in our class. Some men were asking for you.
In **negative** sentences, and quite often in **questions**, we use **any** instead of some:
Do you want any peas ? No I don't like any green vegetables, but I would like some potatoes.
Look back at *Rule 33*, for other uses of *some/any*.

Rule 58   The subject of the verb is often a personal pronoun

This is an important rule, because the personal pronouns are used as the basic subjects when you learn all the different forms of the verb. So you have to be clear what they are:

I	**the first person singular** (sometimes described as 'the person speaking')
YOU	**the second person singular** (sometimes described as 'the person being spoken to')
HE	**the third person singular** (the form used for men, boys, and anything that is masculine (male))
SHE	**also the third person singular** (the form used for women, girls, and anything that is feminine)
IT	**also the third person singular** (the form used for animals, things, objects etc.)
WE	**the first person plural** (So **we** is the *plural* of **I**.)
YOU	**the second person plural** (English uses **you** for both *singular and plural.*)
THEY	**the third person plural** (**They** is the *plural* of **he**, and the plural of **she**, and the plural of **it**.)

Notice that **I** is always written as a *capital letter*.

The above table gives the personal pronouns in their normal order. They are mentioned again in the next rule, where you will see a verb set out with the personal pronouns as subject.

Rule 59   The verb must agree with the subject

This rule looks more complicated than it is.
You already know that the **verb** is the **doing word**, such as:
sees, listens, has been, will go, may come, had been done.

The **subject** is the person or thing that **does** the verb, or carries out the action.
The **subject** may be a **pronoun**.
Remember the **personal pronouns**: *I, you, he, she, it, we, they.*
The **subject** may also be a **noun**.
Remember that **nouns** are **naming words**, the words for people, places and things, like:
the boy, a dog, the fish, Mrs Jones, the congregation, houses, people, India.

You will see how the rule works by looking at the *persons* of a verb written out.

This is the **PRESENT TENSE** of the verb *to talk*. (*Present tense* means *happening now*.)

I talk	You can see at once that there is an **s** on the end of three of these.
you talk	*he talks*, *she talks* and *it talks*.
he **talks**	
she **talks**	This **s** appears on the end of nearly all verbs in the present tense
it **talks**	when the subject is: **he** or **she** or **it**.
we talk	
you talk	It is also there when the subject is a **noun** in the **singular**.
they talk	So we have: *the boy talks; the girl laughs; the dog barks*.

Remember that *you* can be **singular** (only one of you) or **plural** (many of you).
This is why it appears twice in the list.
The difference between singular and plural is important.
When the subject of the verb is a **singular** noun (like: *boy, girl, dog*), then we have the **s** ending.
This makes sense if you think about it: *The boy* is the same as *he*
                                                             The girl is the same as *she*
                                                             The dog is the same as *it*
When the subject is a **plural** noun, there is **no s** ending.
This also makes sense: *The boys, the girls, the dogs* are all the same as *they*.

Sometimes the **subject** of the verb is a large **group of words**.
It is the **main** word that matters in deciding whether it is singular or plural:
the President of the United States of America; the decision of the members of the council;
the art of writing good English; an understanding of nuclear physics are all *singular.*
You can work this out by finding each of the key words: *President, decision, art, understanding.*
So each of these would need a singular verb, and in the present tense that means an **s** on the end.
But: *the marvels of modern science;   arrangements for the opening of the school's new swimming pool;*
the policies of the present government; the distant cries of some unknown and haunted creature
are all **plural**. The key words are: *marvels, arrangements, policies, cries.*
Each of these therefore needs a **plural verb**, and that means **no s** on the end.

Rule 60   Singular collective nouns are followed by singular or plural verbs

If the collective noun stands for the group as a whole - a single unit - then it must have a singular verb.
So: *A flock of sheep grazes on the hillside. The fleet is in port again.*
Parliament meets this week. The entire army is advancing. My team usually loses.
The jury comprises five men and seven women. The party is split on the issue.
The company of angels is praising Thee on high. The crowd was looking ugly.

If the collective stands for the individuals of the group, then a plural verb is sometimes used:
The crew repel/repels the pirates. The choir sing/sings very well. The family come too.
A herd of cattle wander/wanders across the road. The people demand an election.
The police search the premises. The crowd are advancing on the line of policemen.

Police and *people* always have a plural verb.

The **singular** is more usual after the verb *to be* (*is, was* etc.) than a verb of action.
In general, if in doubt, a **singular** verb is much more likely to be right.

Rule 61   Some verbs change their spelling when adding S

As you have learnt under *Rule 59*, when **he** or **she** or **it** or a **singular noun** is the **subject**,
verbs in the present tense must add the letter **s.** Some verbs have to **change** their **spelling** to do this.

Verbs that end in **ch** or **sh** or **s** or **x** or **z** add **es** (instead of just *s*).
Here are some examples:
He reaches the end. The girl catches the ball. She washes her hands. The headmistress teaches us French. The
boy guesses the answer. Time passes slowly. Mum mixes the pudding. The bee buzzes in the flowers.

Verbs that end in **o** also add **es**.
The only examples you are likely to meet are: *go* and *do* (and *undo*).
For example: *Alison goes to bed at eight o'clock, but she does not like it.*
We say the word *does* as if it were spelt *duz* ! Try to remember not to spell it *dose*.
The exception is verbs that end in **oo**, which just add **s**. For example: *The cow moos and the dove coos.*

Verbs that end in **y** change the **y to i**, then add **es**.
Here are some examples:
The plane flies over us. Matthew always cries for nothing. She never replies to my letters.
The verbs before changing the endings in these examples were: *fly, cry* and *reply*.

But verbs that end in **ay** or **ey** or **oy** or **uy** just add **s**.
Here are some examples:
Emily buys a new hat. A criminal disobeys the law. The kitten plays with a ball of wool.
I think Steven enjoys being naughty. He says he didn't do it.
We say the word *says* as if it were spelt *sez* !

The verb **have** does not add *s*. It changes to **has**.
For example: *I have done my homework, but he has not. The dog has a new bone.*

Rule 62   The past tense of most verbs is formed by adding ED

You have already seen how the present tense of verbs works. It is used for actions happening now.
As you would expect, the past tense is used for actions that happened in the past.

For most verbs in English the **past tense** is formed by adding **ed** to the main part of the verb.
If the verb already ends in **e** (like: *move, dance, escape, agree*), simply add **d** to the verb.

Whatever person is doing the action, the past tense is the same. There is no *s* to add anywhere:
I talked, you talked, he talked, she talked, it talked, we talked, you talked, they talked
With noun subjects: *the boy talked, everyone in the room talked.*

This is the simplest of the various tenses in past time. We can use it for any actions in past time, and it is
the tense we normally use for the events in a story.

Rule 63   The past participle of most verbs is also formed by adding ED

Do not be put off by the words *past participle* ("part-iss-ipp-ull").
For most verbs it has the **same form as the past tense.**
You make it by adding **ed** (or **d** if the verb already ends in an **e**) to the present tense.
The past participle has many uses, but for now the main one you need to know follows in *Rule 64.*

Rule 64   The perfect tense is formed with HAVE plus the past participle

The perfect tense is another past tense. Perfect just means 'finished' or 'completed'. So this tense tells you
that the action of the verb is finished.
The perfect tense is formed by the present tense of the verb to **have, plus the past participle** of the main verb.
Remember that the verb **to have** has the form **has** in the third person singular (*he, she, it* and *singular nouns*)

Here is the perfect tense of *talk*:
I have talked, you have talked, he <u>has</u> talked, she <u>has</u> talked, it <u>has</u> talked,
we have talked, you have talked, they have talked.
The same applies with noun subjects: *Politicians **have** talked about it and so **has** the prime minister.*

We use the perfect tense to talk about things which have happened in the past and are finished, and about things
which happened in the past and still apply now.
For example: *I have climbed Mount Everest. He has shaved off his beard.*
I have always wanted a new Rolls Royce (meaning: *I still do want one*).

Notice that the verb *to have* is also used as a verb in its own right meaning *to possess.*
So: *I have a cold* is an ordinary present tense of the verb *to have* - not the perfect of anything.
The past tense and past participle of *to have* is **had**: *I had a cold* (ordinary past tense).
The perfect tense of the verb *to have* is: *I have had* etc.

Rule 65   The pluperfect tense is formed with HAD plus the past participle

The **pluperfect** tense is another past tense. It is further in the past than the perfect. (Its name means "perfect plus".)
It is formed with *had* **plus the past participle**.
It is very simple to form, since *had* does not change at all for the different persons.

Here is the pluperfect tense of *talk*:
I had talked, you had talked, he had talked, she had talked, it had talked,
we had talked, you had talked, they had talked.

The **pluperfect** is used to speak or write about an even earlier time, when you are already speaking
or writing about the past.
For example: *After I had walked* (pluperfect) *half way to the bus stop, I paused* (past tense) *and looked round.*

The **pluperfect** tense of the verb **to have** is: *I had had* etc:
*After he **had had** a look he climbed back down.*

Rule 66   Verbs that end in Y change Y to I before the ED ending

With verbs like *carry, study, deny, horrify,* to make the past tense and the past participle,
you **change** the **y** to **i**, then **add** the **ed** ending.
So the past tense and past participle of these verbs are: *carried, studied, denied, horrified.*

Rule 67   Some verbs double their final consonant when adding ED

When a verb ends in one of the **single consonants**: *b, d, g, m, n, p, r, t* following a *single vowel* (**a, e, i, o, u**),
it **doubles** the **consonant** when **ed** is added to form the past tense or past participle.
Here are some examples: *sob/sobbed   slip/slipped   wrap/wrapped sin/sinned   stir/stirred*
hum/hummed bat/batted   ban/banned   knit/knitted   knot/knotted

The most likely mistake you may make is to apply this rule to verbs which have their own past tense.
The past of *run* is *not runned*, the past of *hit* is *not hitted* etc. (See *Rules 68* to *70* for these verbs.)

Rule 68   Some verbs stay the same in the past form

There are some verbs that have the same present tense, past tense and past participle.
They do **not** form their past tense or past participle in **ed**.

Here is a list of verbs that stay the same, and once again you have to learn them:
cut   hit   let   put   set   split   cost   hurt   burst   thrust   spread

Read also has the same form for all the tenses, but we pronounce the past forms like: *red.*

You will still be able to notice a difference in the third person singular of these verbs though:
He shut the door (past tense); *she shuts the door* (present tense).

Rule 69   Some verbs have an irregular past form

Many verbs in English do **not** form the past tense and past participle with **ed**. Instead they change their form completely. Here is a list of some common ones.

Their past tense and past participle are the same, but they are not formed with **ed**.

Similar sounding words have been grouped together to make learning as easy as possible
- but it is still essential that you do learn them.

Present	Past Tense & Past Participle	Present	Past Tense & Past Participle	Present	Past Tense & Past Participle
bend	bent	meet	met	slide	slid
lend	lent	light	lit*		
rend	rent	get	got	hear	heard
send	sent	shoot	shot	tell	told
spend	spent	sit	sat	sell	sold
		spit	spat	flee	fled
build	built			shoe	shod*
		bring	brought	lay	laid
dream	dreamt*	buy	bought	pay	paid
lean	leant*	fight	fought	say	said (pronounced *sed*)
mean	meant	seek	sought		
		think	thought	have	had
learn	learnt			make	made
burn	burnt	catch	caught		
		teach	taught	win	won
deal	dealt			spin	spun**
feel	felt	bleed	bled	cling	clung
kneel	knelt	breed	bred	fling	flung
		feed	fed	sling	slung
dwell	dwelt	speed	sped*	sting	stung
smell	smelt	lead	led	swing	swung
spell	spelt*			wring	wrung
spill	spilt*	stand	stood	hang	hung*
		understand	understood		
creep	crept			slink	slunk
keep	kept	hold	held		
sleep	slept	behold	beheld	stick	stuck
sweep	swept			strike	struck
weep	wept	bind	bound		
leap	leapt*	find	found	shine	shone
leave	left	wind	wound		
lose	lost	grind	ground	dig	dug

* Words marked with an asterisk can also have the ordinary past tense and past participle ending in **ed**.
Sometimes when there are two alternative forms they may have slightly different uses.
** The past tense *span* does also exist.

Rule 70 Some irregular verbs have a different past tense and past participle

These verbs not only fail to form the past tense or past participle with **ed**, they do not even have the same form for the two.
The past tense is different from the past participle.

The words have been grouped together on the basis of the way they form their past tense and past participle, and these groups should make it easier to learn the different forms.

It is essential once again that you do learn them thoroughly.

Present Tense	Past Tense	Past Participle	Present Tense	Past Tense	Past Participle
rise	rose	risen	swim	swam	swum
arise	arose	arisen	begin	began	begun
write	wrote	written	ring	rang	rung
give	gave	given	sing	sang	sung
drive	drove	driven	drink	drank	drunk
ride	rode	ridden	sink	sank	sunk
choose	chose	chosen	shrink	shrank	shrunk
freeze	froze	frozen			
weave	wove	woven	bear	bore	born/borne
			tear	tore	torn
shake	shook	shaken	swear	swore	sworn
take	took	taken	wear	wore	worn
forsake	forsook	forsaken			
speak	spoke	spoken	blow	blew	blown
break	broke	broken	grow	grew	grown
wake	woke/waked	woken/wakened	know	knew	known
			throw	threw	thrown
tread	trod	trodden/trod	fly	flew	flown
fall	fell	fallen	draw	drew	drawn
steal	stole	stolen	see	saw	seen
bid	bade	bidden			
forbid	forbade	forbidden	saw	sawed	sawn
forget	forgot	forgotten	sew	sewed	sewn**
			sow	sowed	sown**
bite	bit	bitten	show	showed	shown*
hide	hid	hidden	swell	swelled	swollen
beat	beat	beaten	lie	lay	lain
			eat	ate	eaten
run	ran	run			
come	came	come	do	did	done
become	became	become	go	went	gone

*The verb *to show* is also correctly spelt with an **e**: *shew - shewed - shewn.*
**Also notice that *to sow* is used for sowing seed, while *to sew* is used for stitching.

Exercise 13

Read this short paragraph, then answer the questions.

The old magician lifted his magic wand of shining silver and waved it three times above the tall, conical hat which sat lopsidedly on his glistening bald head. Both children shivered in fearful anticipation as they squatted outside the door of the mud hut. They watched his fierce eyes, they heard those cracked lips mutter the ancient spell; they became aware of the shadowy shape that was forming out of the blue smoke of the fire. Their eyes met for a long moment as they asked themselves what manner of creature it was.

(1) Write out all the adjectives in the passage which qualify a noun, and clearly label each as an adjective. Next to each of the adjectives write the noun that it qualifies, and clearly label it as a noun.
(2) Give one word from your list which is a noun acting as an adjective.
Now use that noun to form another adjective, by adding an ending to it.
(3) Give one word from your list which can be either an adjective or a noun.
By adding an ending to it you can form another adjective. What is the new adjective ?
(4) What are the two possessive adjectives in the list ?
(5) What are the two adjectives of quantity in the list ?
(6) What is the only interrogative adjective in the list ?
(7) There is one extra adjective in the passage which is not with any noun. In fact it follows a verb. What is it ?

Exercise 14
Form adjectives from these nouns:
(1) silence   (2) fire   (3) joy   (4) grief   (5) terror
(6) type   (7) humour (8) fortune   (9) history (two)

Exercise 15
Form nouns from these adjectives:
(1) happy   (2) final   (3) moderate (4) silent   (5) impudent
(6) proud   (7) wide   (8) jubilant (9) fierce (two)

Exercise 16
Give the comparative and superlative of the following adjectives:
(1) funny   (2) ancient (3) bad   (4) evil   (5) wry
(6) fat   (7) clever (two forms)   (8) little (two forms)

Exercise 17
Write out these sentences, inserting an article in front of those nouns which need one:
(1) France is bigger than United Kingdom.   (2) Cloth of sari is very fine.
(3) Prime Minister, Mr Major, visited Sri Lanka for Third Test in winter.
(4) There is unicorn in garden eating grass of lawn.   (5) All children are waiting for bus.
(6) I do not like poetry, except poetry of Coleridge.   (7) There was new boy in school today.

Exercise 18

Write out these sentences with the correct forms of the verb. Be careful. Some verbs will need to be changed, but some will not. Also, some sentences may have more than one verb.

(1) The boy talks.   (2) The girls talks.   (3) They all shout.   (4) Cats like mice - for dinner.
(5) The kitten like the ball of wool.   (6) Simon sing his solo so sweetly
(7) You say no, but I say yes.   (8) The barking of the dogs wake him up.
(9) We always tries hard, but we does not always succeed.   (10) I want to see you.
(11) That boy want a good smack.   (12) He flies through the air with the greatest of ease.
(13) Does you like rice pudding ?   (14) We do, but our little brother do not.
(15) Andrew love his old motorbike.   (16) Suddenly he sees the ghost before him.
(17) The two fielders races in but the wicket keeper catch the ball. (18) "Out!" said the umpire.
(19) Arrangements for the opening of the school's new swimming pool seems to be taking up all my time.
(20) The flies fly and the bee buzzes.

Exercise 19

Change these sentences into the past tense.
(1) The baby starts to cry again.   (2) She cries at the top of her voice.
(3) She wants her dinner.   (4) I like school more than anything else.
(5) Soppy Sarah sighs for Cyril Slaithwaite.   (6) Many people die of hunger in Africa.
(7) All the girls study hard for their exams.   (8) Most of them expect to pass easily.
(9) He denies all responsibility for the loss.   (10) I never ask for a second helping.

Exercise 20

Change these sentences into the perfect tense.
(1) He finishes his homework on time.   (2) He behaves very well in class.
(3) The teachers all like him very much.   (4) The other pupils throw things at him.
(5) We are moving into Number Twenty-seven.   (6) Redynke and Co. supply us with our stationery.
(7) What are you implying, Ponsonby ?   (8) Do you enjoy doing these English exercises ?
(9) I always talk to my lettuces.   (10) It makes them grow better in my opinion.

Exercise 21

Change these sentences into the pluperfect tense.
(1) We stay in on Sunday afternoon.   (2) Jonathan, however, decides to go out.
(3) Mary wants to have a game of cricket with him.   (4) They play in the back garden.
(5) As usual, the boy bats first.   (6) The girl does not approve of this arrangement.
(7) So she runs in to bowl at full speed.   (8) The ball hits Jonathan on the head.
(9) He immediately collapses unconscious.   (10) Later he regrets his decision to go out.

Exercise 22

Write down the past tense and past participle of each of these verbs:
(1) write   (2) sing   (3) have   (4) speak   (5) draw   (6) sink
(7) say   (8) fly   (9) find   (10) forget   (11) light   (12) drive
(13) hurt   (14) become   (15) go   (16) arise   (17) dwell   (18) see
(19) saw   (20) beat   (21) like   (22) eat   (23) choose   (24) bring
(25) cry   (26) wrap   (27) cut   (28) strike   (29) play   (30) do

Rule 71   The present participle is formed by adding ING to the basic verb

The **present participle**, like the past participle which you already know all about, is very important for forming other tenses of the verb. These are explained in the following rules. It also has other uses, which we shall come to later on.

So the basic form of the present participle is: *sing - singing, talk - talking, fly - flying.*

Rule 72   Verbs that end in IE change IE to Y before adding ING

This is very simple: we could hardly write *lieing* as the present participle of *lie*, so we write *lying*
There are very few verbs like this: *die - dying, tie - tying, vie - vying, belie - belying.*

Rule 73   Verbs that end in E drop the E before adding ING

This is even more simple, but people very often get it wrong.
The present participle of *move* is **not** *moveing*, and of *have* is **not** *haveing*.
The correct forms are *moving* and *having* - **without** the *e*.

This **does not apply** in two special cases:
(1) Verbs that end in *ee*, which just add *ing* (*agree - agreeing, flee - fleeing*).
(2) Where it is important to avoid confusion:
singe becomes *singeing* to avoid confusion with *sing - singing*;
dye becomes *dyeing* to avoid confusion with *die - dying*.

Rule 74   Some verbs double their final consonant when adding ING

This rule is on the same principle as *Rule 67*, which you should check.
When a verb ends in one of the single consonants: **b, d, g, m, n, p, r, t** following a single vowel, it doubles the the consonant when **ing** is added to form the present participle.

Here are some examples: *throb/throbbing   dip/dipping   trap/trapping   begin/beginning   blur/blurring   drum/drumming   bar/barring   jam/jamming   forget/forgetting   sit/sitting*

Rule 75   The perfect participle is formed with HAVING plus the past participle

The formation of a perfect participle is very simple, so long as you know the past participle.
Put **having** *in front of the* **past participle**; and you have the perfect participle:

Past participle: **talked**   *Perfect participle:* **having talked.**

The perfect participle is used in sentences like: *Having talked most of the night, we finally went to sleep.*

Rule 76   Stress determines double consonants before ING and ED in longer verbs

This rule follows from *Rules 67* and *74*. With short verbs (one syllable), the rule about whether to double the final consonant or not is simple. You double after a single vowel sound. With longer verbs, of two or more syllables, it is not so easy. You only double after a single vowel, if the vowel is the stressed syllable. The part of the word you say most clearly is the part stressed.

Look at these examples, which should make it easier to understand:

offer - offered - offering (no stress on the short *e*, so do not double the *r* for the *ing* and *ed* endings)

refer - referred - referring (the stress is on the short *e*, so the *r* must be doubled)

edit - edited - editing (the stress is not on the short *i*, so the *t* is not doubled)

admit - admitted - admitting (the stress is on the short *i*, so the *t* must be doubled).

There is one further complication. If a longer verb ends in **l**, then the *l* is **always doubled** before adding the *ed* or *ing* ending: *travel - travelled - travelling*, as well as: *propel - propelled - propelling*.

Rule 77   The tenses of the verb TO BE are irregular

You have already seen many examples of verbs with irregular past forms. The verb **to be** also has an irregular present tense. Here are its present, past, and perfect tenses written out in full:

	Present	Past	Perfect
First person singular	*I am*	*I was*	*I have been*
Second person singular	*you are*	*you were*	*you have been*
Third person singular	*he is*	*he was*	*he has been*
	she is	*she was*	*she has been*
	it is	*it was*	*it has been*
First person plural	*we are*	*we were*	*we have been*
Second person plural	*you are*	*you were*	*you have been*
Third person plural	*they are*	*they were*	*they have been*

The names on the left are simply those of the different people or 'persons' who may be doing the particular action. You would be sensible to try to remember them. They are shewn here in their usual order.

It has already been explained that *you* appears twice in the list because *you* can be either singular or plural.

Also notice that *he, she* and *it* all count as *third person singular*.

Remember that **singular nouns** count as **he** or **she** or **it**, and so are followed by **is/was/has been**:

The grass is green, the house was dark and ancient, the journey has been a long one.

Plural nouns count as **they**, and so are followed by **are/were/have been**:

The nights are dark, the knights were bold, these examples have been useful.

The form of the verb with **to** in front of it (*to be, to talk* etc.) is known as the **infinitive**.

The **pluperfect tense** of the verb to be is:

I had been, you had been, he/she/it had been, we had been, you had been, they had been.

Rule 78   Continuous tenses are formed with the verb TO BE and the present participle

You have seen the basic forms of the present, past, perfect and pluperfect tenses already.

There are other tenses, which are used to signify action that **goes on happening** in present or past time. For this reason they are known as **continuous** tenses.
They are formed by various tenses of the verb **to be** followed by the **present participle**.
They are some of the commonest verb forms in the English language.

Present continuous:
I am talking, you are talking, he/she/it is talking, we are talking, they are talking

Past continuous:
I was talking, you were talking, he/she/it was talking, we were talking, they were talking

Perfect continuous:
*I have been talking, you have been talking, he/she/it has been talking, we have been talking
they have been talking*

Pluperfect continuous:
*I had been talking, you had been talking, he/she/it had been talking, we had been talking,
they had been talking*

We use these tenses to describe things that continue happening for some time.
They are not used for definite events or single actions. In writing they are often used to set the scene of the action, while the simple tenses are used for the events.

For example: *I was walking* (continuous) *down the street, when I met* (simple) *Mrs Bonaparte.*
Here the walking continued over a period, but the meeting was a specific single event.
We were all making a noise, and the boys were playing about. Then the teacher came in.
The two verbs in the past continuous tense refer to actions that continued; the arrival of the teacher only happened once, and so has the simple tense.
The sun was shining and the brook babbling merrily over the stones. Children were playing in the fields.
Under the tree sat the shadowy figure of a man. (We start by setting the scene with past continuous verbs, then move onto the story itself with a verb in the past simple.)

The **past continuous** tense is quite often known as the **imperfect** tense.

Notice that the verb **to be** can itself have all these tenses:
I am being, I was being, I have been being, I had been being.
The present and past forms are very common (*I am being good* etc.).
The perfect and pluperfect are rather uncommon.

The only participle with a continuous form is the **perfect participle**.
It is formed with **having been** *plus* the **past participle**: *having been talking.*

34

Rule 79   Some tenses of the verb are formed using the auxiliary TO DO

All the verbs you have seen used to help form other tenses of a main verb are known as **auxiliary verbs**. *Auxiliary* simply means *helper*.

So far the auxiliaries have been the verbs **to be** and **to have**.

This time the auxiliary is **to do**, which is used to form an *emphatic* version of the present and past tenses. *Emphatic* means that you want to make a point of it : *I **did** finish my homework; I **do** want another apple.*

There are other, much more important, uses for these tenses, in forming the *negative* of the verb, which will be explained in full later. (See *Rule 85*.)

Here are the present emphatic and past emphatic of the verb *to talk*.

Present Emphatic:
I do talk, you do talk, he/she/it does talk, we do talk, they do talk

Past Emphatic:
I did talk, you did talk, he/she/it did talk, we did talk, they did talk

The verb **to do** can also be used as a verb **by itself**, with all its own tenses, and with various auxiliaries: *That boy does as he likes. What are they doing ? I have done it now. There is nothing we can do.*
This means that there are tenses of the verb **to do** formed with *do* and *did* as the **auxiliary** verb: *I didn't do it. Then who did do it? What do you do with this? He does not do much work.*

Notice that: *How do you do?* is used as a general formal greeting, especially when someone is introduced. The answer is either: *Very well thank you* or another: *How do you do!*

Rule 80   Another past tense may be formed with USED TO

This tense is used for something which formerly happened frequently or on a regular basis in the past: *She used to walk down here every night. There used to be a great house on that site. I used to suffer from asthma. They never used to visit me, but they do now.*

Be careful with the words **used to**; they may also be a kind of adjective, meaning *accustomed to*: *I am used to long journeys* means *I am familiar with long journeys. I used to go on long journeys* means *I formerly went on long journeys.*

Notice that you can also use: **I was accustomed to** for something done regularly in the past. The rather uncommon verb: *I was wont to* (not 'want' or 'won't'; this is entirely different) means the same thing. So: *She was accustomed to walk in the park every day; and we were wont to meet here there.*

Rule 81   The future tense is formed with WILL and SHALL

You have seen several ways of expressing action in past time: the past tenses of the verb.
There are also, as you would expect future tenses, for things that have not happened yet.

The first of these is the **future** or **future simple**. Its job is to put an event or action in future time.
For example: *She will soon be here. We shall leave at once.*

The second is the **future continuous**, which uses the verb *to be* and the ***present participle*** (like the present and
past continuous tenses). Like the other continuous tenses you have met, the future continuous deals with action
that goes on for some while. For example: *They will be staying for three weeks.   I shall be leaving tomorrow.*

The third is the **future perfect** (sometimes called the *future in the past*), which is a combination of the forms of
the perfect and future tenses. It has simple and continuous forms. It is not very common, and is used when we are
writing in past time and want to connect the action with a future event.
For example: *After I **have** interviewed young Jones, I **shall have** seen thirty-five candidates for the post.*
The future perfect also has its own continuous form.

All these tenses have **shall or will** as their most important auxiliary verb.
It is correct English to use **shall** after **I** and **we** (that is the first person of the verb, singular and plural) ;
and **will** after **you, he, she it, they**, and **noun** subjects (the second and third persons, singular and plural).

The two versions of the future tense and the two of the future perfect of the verb *to talk* are:

Future (simple):
I shall talk, you will talk, he/she/it will talk, we shall talk, they will talk

Future continuous*:*
I shall be talking, you will be talking, he/she/it will be talking,
we shall be talking, they will be talking

Future perfect:
I shall have talked, you will have talked, he/she/it will have talked,
we shall have talked, they will have talked

Future perfect continuous:
I shall have been talking, you will have been talking,
he/she/it will have been talking, we shall have been talking, they will have been talking.

Rule 82   The future tense may also be expressed by GOING TO

The use of *going to* is another way of saying something will happen in the future. There is often an idea of
plan or intention about it. It is used following the verb *to be*:
I am going to talk, you are going to talk, he/she/it is going to talk, we are going to talk, they are going to talk.
For example: *I am going to visit friends tomorrow.* We might also say this using the future continuous as:
I shall be visiting friends tomorrow, with much the same meaning.

Rule 83   Future time is sometimes indicated by the present tense

This is an odd use, but is quite common. The best way to understand it is to look at these examples:
We are going on holiday tomorrow or *We go on holiday tomorrow.*
The doctor is seeing me next week or *The doctor sees me next week.*

Only use it yourself if there are **other words** in the sentence which **show future time**.

Rule 84   WILL and SHALL have different uses

I shall and **we shall** simply tell you that the action of the verb is in the **future**.
You will, he will, she will, it will, they will and **noun** subjects followed by **will** also
simply tell you that the action of the verb is in the **future**.

I will and **we will** tell you that there is a definite **intention or wish** for something to happen.
You shall, he shall, she shall, it shall, they shall and **noun** subjects followed by **shall** also
tell you that there is a definite **wish or intention** for something to happen.

As you can see the second way of using *will* and *shall* reverses the first.
Very few people get this right now, but it is a useful difference, and you should try to remember it.

For example a mother might say to her child: *You will go to bed at eight o'clock* (ordinary future tense).
When the naughty child answers: *I will not*, he is using the verb to express his wish, not just a future event.
His mother will (ordinary future!) probably then reply (as she is very good at English):
You shall go to bed at eight o'clock - expressing her very definite intention.

Rule 85   The negative of the verb is formed with NOT plus an auxiliary

The negative of the verb is when the action does not happen, and **not** is the key word in forming it.

In modern English it is impossible to make a negative with a form of the verb that has just one word
- with the single exception of the verb *to be*.
(Other apparent exceptions, such as: *I do not* are really shortened forms where the main verb is left out.)

You have to use one of the forms where an **auxiliary** or 'helper' verb is there.
So in the present and past tenses this means you cannot use the simple tenses like *I walk, I talked.*
Instead there are two alternative ways of making negatives.

Firstly you can use one of the **continuous tenses**, which already have an auxiliary in one of the
various forms of the verb **to be.**
Secondly you can use the **emphatic tenses** which have **do** or **did** as their auxiliaries. In the negative these tenses
cease to have any strong emphatic sense. They are used as the **direct equivalent** of the **simple tenses.**

The **not** always goes immediately **after the auxiliary** verb.
If there is more than one auxiliary, *not* goes after the first one.

Here are the **negative forms** of the verb *to talk*. Not all of the persons have been shown: only those where there is a difference from the first person singular (the *I* form). You will be able to work out the rest.

Present	I do not talk (he/she/it does not talk)	I am not talking (you/we/they are not talking; he/she/it is not talking)
Past	I did not talk	I was not talking (you/we/they were not talking)
Perfect	I have not talked (he/she/it has not talked)	I have not been talking (he/she/it has not been talking)
Pluperfect	I had not talked	I had not been talking
Future	I shall not talk (you/he/she/it/they will not talk)	I shall not be talking (you/he/she/it/they will not be talking)

Future Perfect	I shall not have talked
	(you/he/she/it/they
	    will not have talked)
		I shall not have been talking
		(you/he/she/it/they
		    will not have been talking)

The negative of the verb to be is *I am not*, *you are not*; *I was not, you were not* etc.

Notice also: *I did not use to* (not *I did not used to*) etc. and *I am not going to* etc.

There are **other** ways of making a sentence **negative** as well as using *not*.
Other negative words include: **no,** *no-one, nobody, nothing, none.*
These words can be used with the *simple forms* of the present and past tenses:
I know nothing. No-one goes there. Nobody returned from the expedition. None of them works.

Rule 86   A double negative makes a positive

If you put **two negative words** in a sentence together, the sentence goes back to being **positive**.
So: *I see no ships* is a negative sentence, and so is: *I do not see any ships* (the more common modern form).
However, *I do not see no ships* means *I do see some ships*.

In the same way people who claim: *I was not doing nothing wrong* may be telling the truth by mistake.
What they said means: *I was doing something wrong.*
Notice that though one of the negative words used in these double negative sentences is generally *not*, the other is very often one of the other negative words. You should avoid using double negatives - intentionally or unintentionally.

You may need to make **other changes** in negative sentences.
For example, we generally use **any** instead of *some*:
I have some money (positive): *I do not have any money* (negative).

Rule 87   Many verbs have shortened forms using an apostrophe

The auxiliary verbs that are used to form the tenses are now nearly always abbreviated (shortened) in spoken English. The shortened forms miss out one or more letters, and the place where the letters were is shown by an **apostrophe**. An apostrophe is a single comma written above the word.

When writing, the shortened forms are often used, especially in letters, notes etc. It is still not very good English to use them in formal essays for school subjects. You can use them if you are writing a story in the first person (*I* as the narrator), and when you are writing dialogue (the actual words people say).

Here are most of the common abbreviated verb forms:

I am - I'm	he is - he's	she is - she's	it is - it's
you are - you're	we are - we're	they are - they're	
I shall/will - I'll	you will/shall - you'll	he will/shall - he'll	she will/shall - she'll
it will/shall - it'll	we shall/will - we'll	they will/shall - they'll	
I have - I've	you have - you've	we have - we've	they have - they've
he has - he's	she has - she's	it has - it's	
I had/would - I'd	you had/would - you'd	he had/would - he'd	she had/would - she'd
it had/would - it'd	we had/would - we'd	they had/would - they'd	

Many other abbreviated forms also exist with *who, what, where, how* etc: *who's* for *who is/who has*; *who'd* for *who had/who would*; *what've* for *what have*; *where'll* for *where will*, and so on.
Notice that the abbreviation for *had* and *would* is the same.
Also *he's/she's/it's* can mean *he is/she is/it is* as well as *he has/she has/it has*.
Nouns may also have similar abbreviated forms: *Mary's not very well* (*Mary is not very well*).

Rule 88   NOT is often joined to verbs in a shortened form

The abbreviation **n't** (*n apostrophe t*) for *not* is very often attached to the end of verb forms to make the negative. As with the abbreviated forms mentioned in the rule before, this should not be used in writing formal essays or compositions.

Here are the common abbreviated forms with **n't**:

is not - isn't	are not - aren't	was not - wasn't	were not - weren't
do not - don't	did not - didn't	has not - hasn't	have not - haven't
shall not - shan't	will not - won't	should not - shouldn't	would not - wouldn't
cannot - can't	need not - needn't	must not - mustn't	ought not - oughtn't

You can often choose whether to use the form with the verb shortened, or the form with the *not* shortened in negative sentences: *She's not coming* and *she isn't coming* mean much the same.

There is **no *abbreviated*** form for *am not*: you have to use *I'm not*.
(*I aren't* is bad English, but when it is turned round to make: *Aren't I ?* it is very common, and may not even be wrong any more. Do not use: *ain't*).
Notice that *cannot* forms one word even when it is not shortened.

Exercise 23

(a) Write out the present participles of each of these verbs:
(1) wring   (2) reply   (3) see   (4) skip   (5) laugh
(6) offer   (7) charge   (8) dye   (9) run   (10) make
(11) defy   (12) untie   (13) leave   (14) free   (15) swing
(16) rub   (17) break   (18) admit   (19) change   (20) swinge

(b) Now, as a revision exercise, see if you can write out the past participles of each verb. You may want to check *Rules 67* to *70* first.

Exercise 24

Fill in the correct form of the verb *to be* in the following sentences, using the tense indicated in the brackets.
(1) Christopher (*present*) a very good boy.   (2) He (*perfect*) good since he (*past*) a baby.
(3) His sister, Alison, (*pluperfect*) always* the naughty one.   (4) I (*future*) thirteen tomorrow.
(5) All those boys who (*past*) on the roof yesterday (*present*) in serious trouble.
(6) (*Infinitive*) or not (*infinitive*) that (*present*) the question.   (7) We (*past*) not responsible for it.
 * You will need to fit *always* in with the verb in this question.

Exercise 25

Change the verbs in these sentences from the simple form to the continuous. So if they are in the present tense make them present continuous; if they are in the past tense make them past continuous, and so on.
(1) I work as hard as anyone else.   (2) I tried to make sense of the English exercises.
(3) They have baffled me completely.   (4) We went down to the shops that afternoon.
(5) She had sung him his favourite song.

Exercise 26

Change the verbs in these sentences from the continuous form to the simple.
(1) I had been waiting there for hours.   (2) What has she been saying about me ?
(3) That baby is always crying.   (4) I was speaking to Auntie Nancy yesterday.
(5) I have been forgetting about that.

Exercise 27

(a) Put these sentences into the future tense. If the present continuous is used, use the future continuous; if the present simple is used, use the future simple. If the past is used, use the future perfect.
(1) He wants another iced bun.   (2) I am going to the pictures.
(3) They waited for an hour.   (4) You have been practising that song for hours.
(5) We are choosing the wallpaper this afternoon.

Which of the sentences in the exercise is already expressing future time ?

(b) Now do a second set of answers using **going to** instead of the future tense.

(c) (1) Write a sentence of your own using **shall** to express **intention**, not just future time.
    (2) Write a sentence of your own using **will** to express **intention**, not just future time.

Exercise 28

Rewrite these sentences using the emphatic form (with *do* or *did*). Keep the same tenses.
(1) I hoped for something better of you.   (2) We want to go to America this year.
(3) They say that Old Joe liked his beer.   (4) Perhaps it killed him in the end.
(5) What were they making in the shed ?   (6) Are you keeping an eye on them ?
(7) You were hiding in the park at the time of the murder; I definitely saw you there; and you did it.

Exercise 29

Change these positive sentences into negative sentences, keeping the same tense for the verb.
(1) They are coming with me.   (2) Jack tries very hard   (3) I have been to France.
(4) I shall go there again.   (5) Derek and Sheila will be getting married in the summer.
(6) Mrs Smith applied for the job.   (7) Terry thinks her application has been successful.
(8) The standard was as bad as last year. (9) She is coming on holiday with us this year.
(10) In Agra we saw the Taj Mahal and visited the Red Fort.   (11) You need a visa to go there.
(12) If he arrives we shall come over.   (13) The man from the gas board has arrived.
(14) It rained last night.   (15) By tomorrow it will have rained for ten days.
(16) Miss Lade from accounts has the file.(17) Miss Pelling gave it to her.

Exercise 30

Explain what is wrong with these two sentences, and rewrite them so that they make good sense.
(1) I has not seen no-one and I does not know nothing.
(2) We do not have no bananas today but we will have any tomorrow.

Exercise 31

Change the verbs that can be changed in the following sentences into their shortened forms.
(1) I am not going to that awful party, and that is final.   (2) What is the matter with you ?
(3) There is nothing wrong with me; you are the one who is in such a bad mood.
(4) I am sorry to hear that Lisa is absent.   (5) I would not do that if I were you.
(6) Even though you could not do any of the exercise, you should have made an attempt.
(7) Jackie said she was planning to give up French, but her mother told her that she was not allowed to.
(8) I cannot imagine who could have done it   (9) Who would have guessed it was the butler ?
(10) Where have you been, you naughty boy ?   (11) I shall only do it if he will not.
(12) She will be wondering what has happened to us.

Exercise 32

Change the shortened forms of the verbs in these sentences into their full forms.
(1) I've never seen anything like it in my life.   (2) Who's a pretty boy then ?
(3) If he'd been in I'd have seen him.   (4) We'd like to know what you've been up to.
(5) I don't know who's been in there, but if I get my hands on him he'll regret it.
(6) You mustn't ever do that again.   (7) I can't say I've ever heard of them.
(8) Sean's in trouble again; I'm told he's been caught stealing apples; he won't get away with it this time.
(9) What'll I say to them if they're there ?   (10) Your mother's been calling you for hours.
(11) If there's any tea in that pot, I wouldn't mind a cup.

Rule 89   The apostrophe is used to indicate missing letters in other abbreviations

There are a few other words you may see, apart from the shortened forms we have mentioned, which have an apostrophe to indicate a letter or letters missed out.

The most common is *o'clock* ('of the clock'). You will see both *'phone* and *phone* used for 'telephone'.
There are also words found in old-fashioned writing or poetry: *e'er* (ever); *e'en* (even).
Children still shout the old fashioned: *'tis* (it is) in the playground, as well as: *'tisn't*, but they are not good English.

Rule 90   The object of the verb receives the action

The object receives the action of the verb.
This means that the object of a verb is the person or thing to which the action of the verb is done.
You know that the subject is the one who carries out the action. The object is in effect the opposite of the subject.

So in: *I sent a letter*, the subject is *I*, the object is *a letter*.
In: *The teacher called the girl* the object is *the girl*.

An object may be a noun or a pronoun, or a group of words standing in for a noun (known as a noun phrase).
In the following examples, the objects are clearly shown:
*Their mother sent **all three boys** to bed.* (Here the object is a noun with its two adjectives.)
*Can you see **him**? Take **me** to your leader.* (In both these sentences the object is a single pronoun.)
*We have destroyed an **entire enemy regiment and all its tanks and artillery**.*
(In this last example the word *regiment* is the basic object, but all the rest is also part of the object: all of it received the action of the verb.)

Notice that the object is only the person or thing that receives the action. It does not include other parts of the sentence, though it can be quite long in itself.

The pronouns change their form when they are the object.
You will already know the object forms: ***me, him, her, us, them*** - and their normal everyday use in this way.
There is more information about how to use pronouns in *Rules 144* and *145*, which you may like to look at now.

Rule 91   Some verbs may have two objects

With some verbs the object comes in two parts. These are verbs which involve changing something.

The object is generally followed by an adjective which describes the change:
We painted the town red. (*The town* is the object, but the adjective *red* is also an essential part of the object.)
The news made us all very gloomy. (*Us all* is the object, but *very gloomy* is needed as part of it to make sense.)

There are similar sentences involving the forms of the verb which you already know as participles:
Can you hear the bomb ticking? (*Bomb* and *ticking* are both parts of the object.)

Rule 92   Intransitive verbs do not have an object

Some **verbs** in English need an **object** to **complete their sense**. Without an object it would not be possible to understand what was meant. These verbs are called **transitive verbs**.

Other **verbs no not need an object**. They make sense by themselves without an object. In some cases they could not possibly have an object. These verbs are called **intransitive** verbs. Remember that the object is what receives the action of the verb; it does not include other pieces of description which may be added to the verb.
Many verbs can be used **both** as **transitive** and **intransitive** verbs (that is, with or without an object).

The verbs in these examples are **transitive**:
I'm just tying my shoelaces. (Without the object, *my shoelaces*, the sentence would not make much sense as:
I'm just tying. The object is needed to complete the transitive verb.)
She has sent hundreds of invitations. (*She has sent* does not mean anything without its object, the invitations.)
Mr Sloggett carefully placed the ball on the tee. (Even with the addition of an adverb, *carefully*, and a piece of additional description, *on the tee*, we do not have a sentence that makes sense without the object - *the ball*.)

The verbs in these examples are **intransitive**:
The baby is sleeping now. (There is not a *thing* that the baby is sleeping; it is just sleeping.)
The stars are shining brightly in the sky. (*Brightly* is not an object; it tells you **how** they were shining; and *in the sky* is not an object; it tells you **where** they were shining. There is nothing in the sentence to tell you **what** they were shining - which is a good job, as that would obviously be nonsense!)
I walked for many miles. (*For many miles* is not the object; it tells you how far. Be careful of sentences like:
I walked a mile. In this *a mile* looks like an object, but is really only adding to the verb, like an adverb.)

Here are some verbs used **both** transitively and intransitively:
Little Johnny cannot write (intransitive, no object), *but Louise can write her name* (transitive; object - *her name*).
The bird was singing sweetly as it flew from branch to branch. (*Was singing* and *flew* are both intransitive.)
The pilot sang a little song, as he flew his plane toward the mountain. (This time *sang* has an object
- *a little song* - and so does *flew* - *his plane*.)

Rule 93   The normal word order in statements is: subject, verb, object

A statement is any sentence which states a fact, rather than giving an order or asking a question. So far we have only really dealt with statements (though there have been some examples of the other two forms of sentence).
As you know, the subject does the action, the verb is the doing word, the object receives the action.
In English we normally order statements in just that way: **subject - verb - object.**

Sometimes we can see this very clearly: *Janet* (subject) *loves* (verb) *John* (object).
Sometimes one of the parts of the sentence, or even all of the parts of it, are long and quite complicated.
Even so, the rule about correct order still applies. You will be able to see it in these two examples:
All of the third year, their teachers and half a dozen parents as helpers (the whole sentence so far has been the subject) *will be attending* (verb - three words) *the performance* (very short object).
We (one word subject) *would like* (verb) tea, *porridge with hot milk, egg, bacon and sausage, toast and marmalade* (all the rest of the sentence after the verb is the object).

This rule is important, because word order makes a great deal of difference:
The boy is chasing the cat. (Game)
The cat is chasing the boy. (Tiger!)

Rule 94   The indirect object states to or for whom the action is performed

An **indirect object** does **not** occur with **all verbs**.
Its main use is with verbs of *giving*, and *telling*.
Where it does occur it can always be replaced with **to** someone or **for** someone.
It is placed in front of the (direct) object.
Because of the existence of indirect objects, it is helpful in sentences where they happen to call the object itself the **direct object**.

The examples will best show you what an indirect object is, and how it is used:
Dad gave Robert a present. (Object, or direct object: *a present* - the thing that was given; indirect object: *Robert* - the one it was given to.) We could rewrite this as: *Dad gave a present to Robert.*
They sent me (indirect object) *a parcel* (direct object).
Have you written him (indirect object) *a letter* (direct object)*?*
You have been telling me (indirect object) *lies* (direct object).
I'll teach you (indirect object) *a lesson* (direct object)*, my lad.*

The indirect object is used when something is done **for** someone, as well as in 'transfers':
Will you make me (indirect object) *a boat* (direct object)*, dad ?*
Come on, Sally, sing us (indirect object) *a song* (direct object).
We could rewrite the second example as: *Come on, Sally, sing a song for us.*

Rule 95   The verb TO BE is followed by a complement

An object is what receives the action of the verb. In the case of the verb **to be** there is no action, and what follows the verb refers to the same person or thing as the subject.
In: *He is a good boy*, *he* and *a good boy* are the same person.

We refer to what follows the verb **to be** as the **complement** (not 'compliment'), because it completes the verb.

The verb **to be** is often followed by an **adjective**, or several adjectives, which tell you more about the subject.
In: *Our new house is very large*, the adjective *large* (and its modifying adverb *very*) add to the meaning of the subject, they are not the object of any action. So they are the **complement** of the verb.

One of the main uses of **adjectives** is as complements of the verb *to be*. Here are some other examples:
That answer is wrong. Sarah Smith isn't very musical. We were all fit and ready. You can't be serious.

There are one or two other verbs which do not perform an action, but rather (like the verb to be) tell you more about the subject, and can therefore be followed by an adjective or other complement.
The main ones are: *seem, appear, get (in some uses), become*, and also: *smell, taste, sound, look, feel.*
He seems rather tired. She appears unhappy. We were all becoming sleepy. That smells good. You sound hoarse. You look dreadful. Do you feel ill? Get well soon!

There are a few **adjectives** which **only** appear **as a complement**, and cannot be used in front of a noun.
The main ones are: *afraid, alive, alone, asleep, awake.*
So we can say: *He is awake*, but not: *'He is an awake boy'.*

Rule 96   The word THERE is used as a general subject of the verb

The use of **there** as a **general subject** of the verb is particularly common when used with the verb **to be**.

There acts as if it were the subject of the verb, but does not mean very much in itself.
The important part is what follows the verb. It would be quite possible to turn the sentence round, and make that part the subject, but in English we do not like putting new information at the beginning of a sentence; we prefer to save it till later.

We decide whether to use the **singular or plural** of of the verb (*is/are, was/were, has been/have been*) after **there**, depending on whether the **main item following** the verb is singular or plural.

Read through these examples, and look at the alternative versions which have been given and which do not use *there*:

There is no need to make such a fuss. (We could make *fuss* the subject and write: *A fuss is unnecessary.*)
There's (there is) a cold wind blowing tonight. (*A cold wind is blowing tonight.*)
There are two possible answers. (*Two answers are possible.*)
There was a strange sensation of dread in the air. (*A strange sensation of dread was in the air.*)
There were three men waiting for me at the airport. (*Three men were waiting for me at the airport.*)

There can be used with various auxiliaries plus the verb *to be*:
There can be no doubt of it.   There must be a thousand of them.
Also notice: *There seems to be...* and *There appears to be...*

You might like to have a look at *Rule 151* for other uses of *here* and *there*.

Rule 97   IT is also used as a general subject of the verb

It is used as the **subject** of the verb with the main event following it, in much the same way as *there*.
It can be followed by other verbs, as well as the verb *to be*, though the verb *to be* is the most common.
It must have a singular verb, since it is one of the pronouns of the third person singular.

Here are some examples to show you how it works:
It is no bad thing to suffer for the cause. (Meaning the same as: *Suffering for the cause is no bad thing.*)
It was terrifying just to hear them talk.   (Meaning: *Just to hear them talk was terrifying.*)
It is forbidden to ride bicycles here.   (Meaning: *Riding bicycles is forbidden.*)
It gives me great pleasure to welcome our speaker today. (Meaning: *I am very pleased to....*)
It requires a man of vision to do the job.   (Meaning: *A man of vision is required...*)

Notice that we use **it** to stand for:
the time: *What time is it ? It's seven o'clock already. It's very late.*
the weather: *What's the weather like. It's awful. It was fine, but now it's raining.*
distances: *It's not far to go now. It was nearly twelve miles to home.*

Rule 98 Orders are expressed by the imperative of the verb

Commands are the second kind of sentence we are dealing with - after statements.

Commands are formed by the imperative of the verb.
The **imperative** is the basic **simplest form** of the verb.
So the imperative of the verb *to talk* is: **talk**; the imperative of *to be* is: **be**.
This is the **only form** of the imperative: it does not change.

Imperatives are sometimes followed by an **exclamation mark** (!) Do not use it too much, however.
Imperatives can give one word sentences, like: *Stop!*
This sort of sentence should generally be given an exclamation mark.

You will probably have noticed that imperatives do not have much sign of a subject. It is sometimes said that the subject is 'understood' to be *you* (i.e. the person being spoken to). Sometimes the subject can be included:
You boy, come here at once! (*You boy* is the subject.)
There can certainly be an object after an imperative, and as in a statement it must follow the verb:
Tidy that terrible mess in your room ! (Everything after *Tidy* is the object.)

Rule 99 Negative orders are expressed by DO NOT plus the verb

In modern English we cannot say *Talk not !* as the imperative form. We have to use the emphatic form of the verb that use the auxiliary: **do**.
The negative imperative of *talk* is: **Do not talk.**
This is the **only form** of the negative imperative: it does not change.

The same rule applies about exclamation marks. Use them sparingly, though they are generally quite a good idea for sentences consisting solely of the negative imperative.

Rule 100 Interjections are shouts or cries

It is convenient to deal with this particular part of speech after imperatives, because orders are also very often exclaimed (shouted, or said loudly).

Interjections are the actual *sounds* we make to express things like amusement, surprise, horror, pain, fear and similar emotions, plus one or two words that have acquired a similar use.
Typical interjections are: *Oh! Ooh! Ah! Ouch! Wow! Alas!*
Sometimes interjections have more than one word: *Oh dear! Dear me! Cor blimey!*

Interjections are nearly always followed by an **exclamation mark**.
Other parts of speech may be shouted out like interjections, and are then also followed by an exclamation mark:
Good! No! Never! Help!

Rule 101   Questions are formed by reversing the subject and auxiliary verb

Questions are the third kind of sentence.

To make a simple question, without using a special question word, we **reverse the order** of the subject and the main auxiliary verb.

You have to use one of the forms where an **auxiliary** or 'helper' verb is there to make this sort of question in modern English. So in the present and past tenses you have to use the emphatic forms (with *do* or *did*), or the continuous form (with the verb *to be*).

The forms with *do* and *did* are the equivalent of the simple present and past tenses, so if you wanted to change: *He talks* into a question it would become: *Does he talk ?* Similarly: *I went* would become: *Did I go ?*

The verb *to be* itself can make questions with its one-word forms, by simply reversing subject and verb. Very rarely you do see this with other verbs (for example: *Have I the right ?* for *Do I have the right ?*).

If a tense is formed with more than one auxiliary verb, you change the order of the subject and the *first* auxiliary.

Here are the main question (interrogative) forms of the verb *to talk*:

Present	**Do I talk?** **(Does he/she/it talk?)**	**Am I talking?** **(Are you/we/they talking; is he/she/it talking?)**
Past	**Did I talk ?**	**Was I talking ?** **(Were you/we/they talking ?**
Perfect	**Have I talked?** **(Has he/she/it talked ?)**	**Have I been talking ?** **(Has he/she/it been talking ?)**
Pluperfect	**Had I talked ?**	**Had I been talking ?**
Future	**Shall I talk?/** **Will you talk?**	**Shall I be talking?/** **Will you be talking?**
Future Perfect	**Shall I have talked ? etc.**	**Shall I have been talking ? etc.**

The interrogative form of the verb **to be** is: *Am I ?   Are you ?   Is he ?* etc.

Other question forms can be made using other auxiliaries, for example:
Can I go now ?   Would you like a cup of tea ?   Must we answer all the questions ?
Also notice: *Did I use to* etc. and *Am I going to* etc.

Noun subjects behave just like the pronouns used in the examples above.
So: *Mrs Smith was talking* becomes, as a question: *Was Mrs Smith talking ?*
The members of the district council have decided becomes: *Have the members of the district council decided ?*

Notice that in questions, just as in negatives, *some*, and *something, somewhere* etc. quite often change to *any* (*anything, anywhere* etc.). For example: *He wants **some** ice-cream* becomes *Does he want **any** ice-cream ?*

Rule 102   In negative questions NOT follows the subject in the full forms

In the full form of negative questions, the **not** goes **after the subject** in the reversed order.
Here are the negative forms of the tenses shown in *Rules 78* and *79*.

Do I not talk ?   Am I not talking ?   Did I not talk ?   Was I not talking ?   Have I not talked ?
Have I not been talking ?   Had I not talked ?   Shall I not talk ?   Shall I not have talked/been talking ?

Similarly with other auxiliaries we would have: *Can I not come to the ball ? Aren't we going to the ball?*
Would you not prefer coffee ?   Did you not use to like coffee ?   Should we not be going now ?

The rule applies with noun subjects: *Has Alderman Foodbotham not spoken about this incessantly ?*

Rule 103   Negative questions normally use the short form of the verb with N'T

The full forms described in *Rule 102* are not very common, and tend to be used only for emphasis, or when very correct and precise writing is required.

The shortened equivalents are nearly always used in speech:

Don't I talk ?
Didn't I talk ?
Wasn't I talking ?
Haven't I talked ?   Haven't I been talking ?
Hadn't I talked ?   Hadn't I been talking ?
Shan't I talk ? (and: Won't you talk ? etc.)   Shan't I be talking (Won't you be talking?)
Shan't I have talked/ have been talking ?

Notice there is no short form for: *Am I not talking ?* You can say: *Aren't you talking ?   Isn't he talking ?* etc.,
but: *Aren't I talking ?* is **not** very good English (though you often do hear people saying : *Aren't I...?*).

Rule 104   Negative Questions are loaded to expect the answer YES

This is a rule about how to use negative questions. If you think about it, it seems rather odd that we should need negative questions at all. However, they fulfil a precise purpose.

When we ask an ordinary question we are simply asking for information.
Are you coming with us ? could equally be answered by *yes* or *no*.

If we make it a negative question:
Aren't you coming with us ? we are expecting the answer to be: *Yes, of course I'm coming with you.*

When the form of words we use is designed to influence the answer in this way it is called **loaded**.

Loaded questions (negative questions) of this sort can cause some doubt about what a simple *yes* or *no*
as the answer means. In practice *yes* means agreement with the direction of the loading, *no* means disagreement.

Rule 105   Loaded questions may be formed by adding a question to a statement

The way we do this is to say or write something as a **statement** (i.e. with the normal order of subject first, then verb), but then to **add a short question** to the end of it. The question part at the end is negative if the main statement is positive, and positive if the main statement is negative. It is easiest to understand this from examples:

You are coming with us (positive statement), *aren't you ?* (negative question tacked on to the end).
If you think about it, you will realise that once again this way of asking a question is loaded to suggest the answer:
Yes of course I am coming with you...
Notice how it works in these other examples: *Jenkins will vote for me, won't he ? He does take sugar, doesn't he ?*
The price of cod is very high, isn't it ?   We can rely on your support, Anne, can't we ?

You aren't coming with us (negative statement), *are you ?* (positive question tacked on to the end).
This time, if you think about it, you will realise that the question is loaded the opposite way, to suggest the answer:
No, of course I'm not coming with you...
Notice how it works in these other examples: *They haven't already gone, have they ?*
The government hasn't been defeated, has it ?   We needn't wait any longer, need we ?

Remember that the answer expected to a loaded question, is not necessarily the answer which will be given:
You are coming with us, aren't you ? may get the (unexpected) answer: *No, I don't think so this time....*
You aren't coming with us, are you ? may get the (unexpected) answer: *Yes, perhaps I will for a change...*

Rule 106   Questions may be formed with question words

Most questions formed with question words reverse the order of subject and verb. For example:
Statement: *He is going.*
Question by simple reversal: *Is he going ?*
Question with question word: *Where is he going ?   When is he going?   Why is he going ?*

The main question words of this type are: when   where   why   how

How is often joined with another word: **How much   how many   how often**
For example: *How much is that doggy in the window ?   How many times must I tell you ?*

Rule 107   If the question word is the subject, the order is not reversed

This sort of question happens when the word used to ask the question is the **subject**.
The most common word used in this sort of question is: who
For example: *Who is coming ?   Who has made that terrible mess ?   Who was talking ?*

Sometimes other question words are used as the subject.
Look at the examples below. In each case the first alternative has the question word as the subject, and the second one has a different subject. So in each case the first one has no reversed word order, but the second one does.
What made you do it ? (**What** is the subject.) But: *What have you done ?* (**You** is the subject: word order reversed.)
Which of you spilt this ink ? (**Which** is the subject.) But: *Which of them do you want ?* (**You** is the subject.)
How many are coming with me ? (**How many** is the subject.) But: *How many can we take ?* (**We** is the subject.)

Rule 108   WHO, WHICH and WHAT have special uses in forming questions

These three question words are special as they can be used either as the **subject** or the **object** of the questions they are asking. You have already seen some examples of this in the rule before, but there is another important complication that causes many difficulties.

Who is a pronoun (an interrogative pronoun), and like other pronouns you have already seen, it has a different form when it is the object. The **object** form of *who* is **whom**. So it is necessary to decide if the pronoun is acting as the subject (performing the action of the verb), or if another word or group of words is the subject.

Study these examples to see how *who* and *whom* are correctly used:
Whom did you wish to see ?   *Whom has he chosen for the job ?*   *For whom were you waiting ?*
Who wishes to see me ?   *Who has got the job ?*   *Who is that waiting out there ?*

Now you know the rule, you can be told that it no longer matters very much. When we are speaking we nearly always use **who** *instead of* whom for the object. You should use *whom* in serious, formal writing, but only if you are quite sure it is correct. So the first set of examples above could, without being wrong, appear as:
Who did you wish to see ?   *Who has he chosen for the job ?*   *Who were you waiting for ?*

Whose is another form of *who* that can be used as a question word. It means *of whom*, or *belonging to whom*.
For example: *Whose is this ?   Whose writing was the best ?   Whose picture are you drawing ?*

Which can also be an interrogative pronoun, and can also be the subject or object:
Which do you want ? (Object.)   *Which will win the race ?*   (Subject.)

Which is more often used as an interrogative adjective.
This simply means it is joined to a noun when it asks its question:
Which boys have finished their homework ?   Which girls has Mrs Spottiswood punished ?

What has its own uses as an interrogative pronoun or adjective; and it can be subject or object:
What do you want ?   What's the matter ?   What time is it ?

It is also used in **What kind of** ? ; **What** *is something* **like** ? and **What......for** ?
What kind of man are you anyway ?   What is she like as a mother ?   What are you doing that for ?

Whatever is used to ask questions intended to show surprise: *Whatever is the matter ?*

It is sometimes difficult to decide when to use **which** and when to use **what**.
In many cases there is not much difference between the two, but generally we use **which** when we are asking about something which we already know about, a particular item rather than a general one. We use **what** when we are asking about something on which we have no information, and are asking a general question.

Here are three examples of dialogue which may help:
What can I get you, sir ?   I'll have some pudding please. Which of them would you like, sir ?
What is your house like ?   It's one of the old ones in Wimpole Street. Oh yes, which one ?
What sort of books do you like ?   I like historical novels. Which do you prefer, Scott or Jane Austen ?

Rule 109   Statements may be used to ask questions

By putting a question mark after a statement, without changing the order of the words at all, you can turn it into a question. In spoken English we change the way we stress words from statement to question, and the question mark at the end is enough to tell us that a particular statement needs to be said like a question. This usually means (among other things) that we make our voices go up towards the end of the sentence, and put more stress on the auxiliary verb.

So: *Lisa is voting for me in the election ?* and: *You are behaving yourselves in there ?* are both perfectly good questions, without changing any words around.

You might also have noticed that they are rather like loaded questions, expecting the answer *yes*.
We could have put: *isn't she ?* onto the first one and: *aren't you ?* onto the second without changing the meanings.

If the statement is negative, then the loading tends to be towards the answer *no*, as in the following examples:
You're not rioting in that cloakroom?   The mayor isn't opening the fete this afternoon ?
Here we could have added: *are you ?* to the first one, and: *is he ?* to the second without changing the meaning. However, the same statement used as a question can also be employed to express surprise, and that may affect the expected answer.

Another way of making statements into loaded questions is to put the word: **Surely** at the beginning.
For example: *Surely you are coming with us ?* This question is, of course, loaded to expect the answer: *yes*.

To make a negative loaded question with surely, we simply make the statement negative:
Surely you are not coming with us ?

Rule 110   Shortened forms of the verb are often used in answers to questions

When answering questions with **yes** or **no**, if we add a subject and verb, we use the **first auxiliary** of the verb, **not** the whole verb. So you might say we miss out the main part of the verb.

Look at these examples:
Are you coming with us? - *Yes, I am/No, I'm not.*   *Do you want any pudding ?* - *No, I don't/Yes I do.*
Didn't you understand - *Yes, I did/No I didn't.*   *You will write, won't you?* - *Yes, I shall* (or *Yes I will*).

In the second example above, it would be **wrong** to answer: *Yes, I want.*
You must use the auxiliary unless you are going to give a fuller answer.
The answer need not be much fuller: *Yes, I want some* is correct.
Notice that in the answer *any* changes to *some* - the reverse of the process mentioned at the end of *Rule 101*.
In the third example, *Yes, I understood*, using the simple past tense, would also be correct.

When the verb *to be* by itself (not as an auxiliary) is the verb in a question, it can also be used by itself in a shortened form of the answer.
For example: *Were you a good girl today ?* - *Yes, I was.*   *Is Jonathan upstairs ?* - *Yes, he is.*

Rule 111   Shortened forms of the verb are used to avoid repetition

If we have used a verb once in a sentence, and then want to mention the same action again, we generally prefer just to **use an auxiliary**, and leave out the verb itself. The auxiliary used is generally a part of the verb **to be** or the verb **to do**. It does not matter if there was no auxiliary when the main verb was first used. One can still be inserted in place of the second appearance, so long as it is in the right tense. So if the main verb being left out should be in the past tense, it will be necessary to have a past tense auxiliary in its place.
For example:
He said he would come, but I don't think he will. (*Will* is short for *will come*.)
Jack always wins, but I never do. (*Never do* is used instead of *never win*.)

In addition to missing out most of the verb, we often also miss out the **object**, or other pieces of additional information, when they are the same as ones that have already been stated:
I've done my homework, but Jenny hasn't (missing out the verb *done* and the object *her homework*).
You can go to the park with Emma Puddle if you want to, but I'm not. (*Not* is short for: *not going to the park*.)

Sometimes we can miss out a great deal of the sentence, when it would repeat what has already been said.
This can happen in alternative choices offered:
Do you want to come to the pictures with me or not? In this example, *or not* stands for: *or do you not want to come to the pictures with me*. **Or not** is always used in this way.
We also use **so** plus **subject and auxiliary reversed** to avoid much repetition:
*Robert is particularly fond of apple pie and custard, and **so am I**.*
*They frequently work for twelve hours at a time when they are busy. **So do we!***

Rule 112   The infinitive is formed with TO and the basic verb

The **infinitive** of the verb is the simplest or **basic form**, and does not change.
We state the infinitive with **to** in front of it: *to talk, to write, to do, to think, to be.*

There is also a much less common form of the infinitive in past time.
It is known as the **perfect infinitive**, and we might think of it as the basic form of the perfect tense.
It is formed by : **to have** plus the **past participle**.
So: *to have talked, to have written, to have done, to have thought, to have been.*

Rule 113   Some auxiliary verbs have only a single form

This rule is mainly to make sure that you do not put the present tense **s** ending for the third person singular, or any past tense endings (such as **ed**), or the **ing** ending for a present participle on the following verbs. They have different uses but they always stay the same. These verbs are not used to form the different tenses like the other auxiliaries we have dealt with so far. You will see their special uses in the following rules.
These are the verbs: **can**   and   **could**
                                  may   and   **might**
                                  should and   **would**
                                  must.
These verbs are sometimes known as **modal** verbs, and since that is a convenient name for them, it is used when they are mentioned as a group - in the next rule for example.

Exercise 33
In these sentences write out separately the subject, object and verb, and clearly label each.
(1) Everyone must do maths and English. (2)   Seventy percent of our pupils have obtained a high grade.
(3) She should have been reading a book. (4)   You can see the cliffs of the French coast.
(5) Mr Battacharya, the acting chairman, delivered an excellent keynote speech.

Exercise 34
In these sentences, change the order so that the subject becomes the object, and the object becomes the subject.
(1) All the other girls dislike Ermintrude Cholmondeley.
(2) A regiment of enemy soldiers had captured one of our tanks.
(3) Parliament has decided to purge the civil service of undesirable elements.
(4) Mrs Cadwallader accompanied her son, Arthur, to the eisteddfod.
(5) The boys in Form Three were eating the fish from the school pond again.

Exercise 35
Read this short passage carefully, then answer the following questions:

> We all wrote Mr Grimaldi a letter, and sent him it by the messenger. That same night
> everyone packed, and then left the encampment. We knew he would surely be angry
> when he received our message, but we were not afraid. By then we would have gone.
> We could travel ten miles before the morning. He would never catch us then.

(a) What two words are used as indirect objects ? Which verb does each of them follow ?
(b) Give two verbs that are used intransitively in the passage.
(c) What is the object of *sent* in the first line and *left* in the second ?
(d) What is the subject of *left* in the second line, and *catch* in the last line ?
(e) Give the two words in the passage used as complements of the verb *to be*.
(f) What is the object of *travel* in the last line ?

Exercise 36
Rewrite these sentences using **there** as the subject of the verb **to be**.(You may have to make several changes.)
(1) A cold wind is blowing tonight.   (2) A nasty-looking fellow was asking for you.
(3) A vast creature lurked at the threshold.   (4) Serious floods have occurred in the Punjab.
(5) His presence in Monte Carlo cannot now be doubted.

Exercise 37
Rewrite these sentences using **it** as the subject of the sentence and making any other necessary changes.
(1) Welcoming our speaker today gives me great pleasure.   (2) Running in the corridor is forbidden.
(3) Writing to Great Aunt Agatha is always very difficult.   (4) A completely new approach is needed.
(5) The problem is not particularly difficult.

Exercise 38
Rewrite these sentences to mean the same thing, but without using **it** or **there** as the subject.
(1) There has been a report of another robbery. (2) It was a dark and moonless night.
(3) It is very pleasant doing English exercises. (3) There was no other candidate available for the post.
(5) There is no escape for you, Count Oldenburg.

Exercise 39

Change the following commands from positive to negative or negative to positive.
(1) Eat that ice-cream, Billy (2) Please talk to me, Angela.   (3) Stop now!
(4) Do not wait for me.   (5) Do not write anything in this space.

Exercise 40

Change these sentences from statements into questions.
(1) She is talking to Josephine. (2) You have seen the Parthenon. (3) They have been good today.
(4) We can go now.   (5) Mrs Kropotkin arranged the flowers in the church.
(6) Those boys have been frightening Soppy Cecil again.   (7) You did last night's homework.
(8) It will really have been twenty-seven years next week.   (9) Fred wants some pudding.
(10) The journey from Derby to Swindon usually takes more than two and a half hours.

Exercise 41

(a) Make these statements into negative questions, using the full form of the negative.
(1) I have waited long enough.   (2) Jackie is not coming with us.
(3) The children were playing in the garden.   (4) We shall be going to the theatre this evening.
(5) Cousin Cynthia plans to come with us.   (6) She is very good at maths.
(7) The rain in Spain falls mainly on the plain. (8) Jenkins wanted to see Mr Mireworthy.
(9) Three of the patients had been complaining of severe headaches.
(10) The match against Slugborough Athletic should have been arranged for next Friday.

(b) Now rewrite each of your answers to the first exercise, this time using the shortened form
of the negative to make the question.

(c) Once again using the sentences, make each one into a loaded question expecting the answer *yes*
by adding a shortened negative question at the end.

(d) Still using the same sentences, now make each one into a question expecting the answer *no* by adding
a shortened question at the end. You need to make the statement negative and then add a positive question.

Exercise 42

Put the correct question word into each of these sentences:
(1) Which/what one do you prefer ?   (2) Who/what/why are we waiting ?
(3) What/why are we waiting for ?   (4) For who/whom are we waiting ?
(5) Who's/whose book is this ?   (6) Which/what boys are responsible for this ?
(7) How much/how many do they cost ? (8) Which/what can I do to help ?
(9) Who's/whose coming swimming ?   (10) Whichever/whatever are they doing ?

Exercise 43

Give a short form answer to each of these questions, using first **yes** and then **no**:
(1) Is he coming ?   (2) Are you responsible for this mess ?
(3) Have they arrived yet ?   (4) Don't you like Elizabeth much ?
(5) They did reply, didn't they ?

RULE 114 Modal verbs are usually followed by the basic form of the verb

This rule is about the verbs just listed in *Rule 113*: **can, could, may, might, should, would, must.**
The main verb for which they are the helpers or auxiliaries is usually in the simplest possible form:
(as in the infinitive, but without the *to* in front of it). This form does not change whatever the use.

You can see how it works in these examples:
I can do it. Can you read that chart on the wall ?   The whole class can recite the seven times table.
Could you help me with this please.   I may speak to her later. You shouldn't go in there.
We would like to see the manager, please. It must be difficult to understand.

All these auxiliaries may also be followed by the **perfect infinitive** (*without* to) to indicate that the event
happened in past time. Again, the examples will show you how it works:
I could have done it once, but I can't any more.   She could have bought the blue one or the red.
We may/might have been to Frankfurt that year, but I'm not sure. They must have been mad.
I could have sworn I saw him.   You shouldn't have done that. Would you have done it ?

One other form sometimes follows these auxiliaries: **be** plus the **present participle** of the main verb.
You can see how this works in these examples:
She may be coming to the party.   We could be wasting our time

Notice that these auxiliaries form negatives and questions in exactly the same way as other auxiliaries:
Can you fix it ?   You couldn't do it.   Shouldn't that be in the cupboard ?
The negative form of *can* is written **cannot** or **can't.**

Rule 115   CAN and COULD have several uses

The main use of **can** is to indicate the **ability** to do something.

For example: *I can just see the mountains.   Little Jane can ride a bike now.*
Since his accident, he cannot speak properly.   Can you reach that packet on the top shelf ?

Can is also used to indicate that something is **possible.**

For example: *That Mavis Greenspawn can be a real pest. It can sometimes rain for weeks.*
Can Jack really have been responsible ?   You can't be serious.

Could is used as the **past tense** of **can** to indicate **ability** and **possibility** in past time.

For example (ability): *When we reached the top we could just see the people on the ground.*
Jason could run faster than me last year, but he can't any more.   I couldn't help it, honestly.

For example (possibility):
Once upon a time you could walk from England to France.   Jerry couldn't help it.
I could have been killed by that lorry.   They could still be waiting at the bus stop.
Notice *be + present participle* in the last example.

Rule 115 cont.

Can and **could** are both used for **requests**.

Could is a polite way of asking for something, and is very common, and completely correct
For example: *Could I see you for a moment, Mr Droople ?   Could you turn that radio down, please?*
Notice that the form of these requests is a question, so they need a question mark.

Can is also used to ask for things, but these requests are more like orders, and not quite such good English.
For example: *Can you turn that noise off ?   Can't you two stop arguing?*

Can is also used (much more courteously) for offers of assistance.
For example: *Can I get you something for that headache ?   Can I be of assistance to madam ?*

Notice that *can* and *could* may both be used for future as well as present time:
I can arrive tomorrow.   I could do it next week.

You should read the next two rules carefully as well as this one for the difference between *can* and *may*.

Rule 116   MAY and MIGHT have several uses

May is used for **permission** and **requests** for permission to do something.

For example: *Please may we go now, Miss ?   You may go as soon as the room is tidy.*
The common people may not enter the palace.   May I take my holiday next month ? (Future time.)

May and **might** are both used to indicate **possibility**.

For example: *John may be upstairs in his room. He might go to the dance tonight* (future).
I may be going too (be + participle). *She might have caught the seven fifteen* (perfect infinitive without *to*).
There does not seem to be any hard and fast rule about whether to use *may* or *might* in modern English,
so simply use the one that sounds right to you.

Rule 117   CAN and MAY should be used slightly differently

Most children in school used to learn this from teachers making jokes when a pupil asked: *Can I go to the toilet ?*
The teacher would then answer: *I don't know. Can you ?* The point of this is that the pupil should have said:
May I go to the toilet ? because he was asking permission, not asking whether he had the ability !

This rule is often ignored or forgotten now, and it is no longer very bad English to say: *Can I* ? when
you are asking for permission, especially if you include 'please' in the sentence. When you are writing an
essay or a formal letter, however, try to stick to the rule.
Here are a couple of examples to illustrate it:
May I see the Headmaster ? is strictly correct, but: *Can I see the headmaster ?* would be acceptable.
You may speak now is correct: *You can speak now* is acceptable.

Rule 118   WILL and WOULD, and SHALL and SHOULD have several uses

You already know the uses of *shall* and *will* in forming the future tense:
Shall is used after **I** and **we** (except in Scotland and Wales where *I will* and *we will* are normal).
Will is used after **you, he, she, it, they**; and after **noun** subjects.
In spoken and much written English, these distinctions are lost by the use of: *I'll, you'll* etc.

You may also remember that if we reverse the way the pronouns of the future tense work, *will* and *shall* can be used to express intention: *I will go to the cinema with Joe* means that I am going whatever happens.
You shall do as you are told has the suggestion of a threat about it, rather than just a future tense.

Would is used as a **past** tense of **will/shall**.
For example: *Little Timmy won't go to school* (present): *Little Timmy wouldn't go to school* (past).
She would always put a light in the window is an example of *would* used to show something that happened regularly.

The use of *I should* and *we should* as the past tense of *I shall* and *we shall* is now uncommon. To avoid confusion with the other meanings of *should*, we now normally use *I would* and *we would* as the past tense.
You should also look at *Rule 114* for another way *I would* is used in past time.

Would is used for **unreal** possibilities.
For example: *I wouldn't write the boss a letter. In your place, I would go and see him.*

Would or **should** may be used in phrases like: *I shouldn't wonder if... I wouldn't be surprised if...*

Would is used for polite **requests** and **offers**.
You have already seen that *can*, and especially *could* are used in this way (*Rule 115*), and *would* is similar.
For example: *Would you come this way, sir ?   Would you care for another biscuit, Horace ?*

Would + mind is also used for requests: *Would you mind using the other door ?*

Would + like is used more for an offer than a request: *Would you like to see upstairs now ?*
It is also used when asking for something: *I would like another cup of tea, please.*
(In ordinary spoken English we might well say: *I wouldn't mind another cup of tea.*)

Should is used for giving **rules**, general instructions or advice.
It is not quite as direct as a simple imperative command, but still has the idea of getting someone to do something, or at least saying what is and is not allowed or advisable.
For example: *You should never play with matches.   Children should be seen and not heard.*
You shouldn't have done that.   Should we ask that awful Snood woman ?   We should be going now.

Should is used for **likely events**.
For example: *It should be in the top drawer.   The flight should be arriving this afternoon.*
They should have arrived by now. (In the last example the likely event has not happened.)

Rule 119   MUST has several uses

The main use of **must** is for giving **instructions**.

Sometimes **must** is stronger than a simple imperative, as it stresses the importance of the order.
Must is also more general. The **imperative** says: *Do something now!*   **Must** says: *Always do something!*
For example: *You must change your clothes regularly.   All children must use the correct peg.*
Evidence of exemption must be provided to the proper authorities.   We mustn't open them till Christmas.

Sometimes **must** is used in a weaker way, rather like **should**: *We must be leaving now.*

Must is also used to say that something is **certain**, or at least very likely.
For example: *You must be very upset.   It must have been 1963 when we met.*
That can't be right; you must have made a mistake.
Notice how **can** and **must** mean much the same in the last example

Also notice that we say things like:
I must be mad or *you must have dreamt it*, when something unlikely happens.

Rule 120   There are several other verbs expressing obligation

The verb **to have to** is used in much the same way and with the same meaning as **must**.
It is not a modal verb, because it is formed with **have**, which does change its form:
He has to stay in at break. We had to reply at once. I have had to send them back. You don't have to go.

There is another form of *have to*: **have got to**: *I've got to go; he had got to escape.*
This is very common in spoken English, but is not regarded as quite correct in formal written English.

The very odd verb **had better** is used to give advice or recommendations, rather like a stronger form of should.
It is a **modal verb** because it does not change its form, and it should really only be used in present or future time.
It is followed by an **infinitive *without* to**.
Rather similar is **had best**, which is less common, and means much the same.
Here are some examples: *You had better stop it. They'd better not have done it.*
She'd better not show her face in here again. We'd best be going now.

The verb **to need** has several meanings.
When it is used simply ***with an object*** (for example: *A hungry man needs food*), it means ***to lack***, or ***to require***.
It can be used in much the same way followed by an infinitive as **to need to**: *A thirsty man needs to drink.*

Used in this way **need** is a perfectly ordinary verb, but in the negative: **need not** or **needn't**, it becomes a modal verb, and does not change its form: *He **need** not do it; she **needn't** do it either* (**not** *needs not* or *needn't*).

Ought is a **modal verb**, and therefore has only one form. It is used rather like **should**, for giving advice and **recommendations**, and also to say that something is **likely**. It is followed by the **infinitive with *to***:
You boys ought not to be in here. There ought to be a law against it. Surely we ought to be there soon.

Rule 121   Many verbs may be followed by another verb in the infinitive

You have already seen *need to* as one simple example.
There are also: *want to, wish to, like to, love to, prefer to, hope to, try to, attempt to, seek to, choose to, decide to, prepare to, pretend to, claim to, seem to;* and many others.
Look at the following examples:
Mr Pritchard wants to speak to David. Would you like to come with us ?
They have decided to abstain. Prepare to meet your doom!

Some of these words are very often followed by the verb **to be** plus an adjective:
He claims to be my long-lost cousin. Pretend to be dead. You seem to be lonely.

Notice that the verb *learn* is sometimes followed by *how to*; and verbs like *know* and *understand* must have *how to* rather than just the plain infinitive. For example:
She is learning how to dance. I know how to speak Hindi. Do you understand how to do it ?

Rule 122   The verb TO BE plus an adjective may also be followed by an infinitive

In some cases the verb **to be** followed by an **adjective** or a **participle** and **then the infinitive** of another verb forms a kind of compound verb.

Two of the commonest are: *to be able (unable) to*, and *to be ready to*:
I am unable to agree. The enemy were able to attack the column. The general had been ready to surrender.

There are others which tend only to appear in forms starting with **it** (See *Rule 97*):
It is essential to reduce expenditure. It is necessary to make deep cuts. It is advisable to raise taxes.

Rule 123   Some parts of the verb may be used as nouns

The parts of verbs that can be used in this way are two forms which you already recognise.
The first of these is the **present participle** (ending in **ing**).
When this is used as a noun, it is known as a **verbal noun**.

The other form of the verb that can be used as a noun is the **infinitive**.
The infinitive is the basic form of the verb, with **to** in front of it.

These two parts of the verb can be used like most other nouns.
They may be the subject of the sentence: *Driving a car is easy. To drive well is much more difficult.*
They may be the object: *I hate driving; I prefer to walk. I would not want to have missed that.*
Notice that it is the perfect infinitive which is used in the last example.

You have already seen the infinitive used as the object in the preceding two rules.
Whenever a verb is followed by an infinitive in this particular way, the infinitive is acting as the object of the verb.

Rule 124   The possessive of verbal nouns ending in ING is formed with OF

The possessive form using *apostrophe s* is **not** normally used with verbal nouns.
So we say: *the art of writing*, not *writing's art*.
Other examples are: *There are many styles of writing. What is their method of selecting a new candidate? The sound of singing came to their ears. He is consumed by the fear of dying.*

There is **no possessive** form that can be used with an **infinitive**.

Rule 125   Verbal nouns ending in ING rarely have an article

In most cases these nouns are used without any article.

However, occasionally a verbal noun is found with the indefinite article, when a single example is referred to, but no details are given or known about it: *The police suspected that there had been **a** killing.*
Similarly, if it is a particular example which has already been mentioned, or about which some details are known, then the definite article may be used: *The police suspected him of **the** recent killings.*

When a **verbal noun** in **ing** is followed by **of**, it must have a **definite article**.
This part of the rule appears difficult, but is not really. The examples will help to explain it:
***The** writing **of** good English is far from easy.*
Because *writing* is followed by a possessive (*of good English*), there must be a definite article (*the*) in front of it.
We could just as easily have said: *Writing good English is far from easy.*
In that case it would be **wrong** to insert **the** in front of the verbal noun, because there is **no** *of* involved.
You cannot in English say: *the driving a car, the reading a book* etc. If a verbal noun is directly followed by another noun (which is in fact acting as its object) it very rarely has an article.

An infinitive cannot have any article, and may be followed by *of* without any special problems:
I used to dream of meeting you.

Rule 126   Some verbs are generally followed by verbal nouns ending in ING

As already mentioned in *Rule 121*, some verbs are often followed by an infinitive (*to pretend to work, to want to go, to like to play* etc.).

Other verbs are generally followed by a **verbal noun** ending in **ing**: ***stop, cease, finish, start, begin, commence*** (and other verbs meaning *stop* or *start*) are probably the commonest examples:
You may start writing now. Stop complaining.

Some of the verbs mentioned in *Rule 121* may take a **verbal noun** as an alternative to an infinitive:
To love and ***to like*** are probably the commonest: *I love swimming; I like to swim.*
Learn can also be followed by either:
She is learning (how) to dance/ she is learning dancing.

Rule 127   Nouns can be formed from verbs

As you have seen, parts of the verb may be used as nouns. It is also possible to form nouns from verbs.

Abstract nouns are very commonly formed from verbs by adding one of these three endings: **tion, sion, ation**.
However, there are also many other endings added to verbs in much the same way to form nouns.
Here are some examples, giving the verb and the noun formed from it:
form - formation, create - creation, provide - provision, move - motion, impose - imposition,
succeed - success, please - pleasure, judge - judgement (or, in the law: *judgment*), *enter - entrance.*

Often, especially with short, simple words, there are two slightly **different forms,** one of them a noun,
the other a verb:
weigh - weight, speak - speech, live - life, think - thought, sing - song.

Sometimes the same word can be used as both noun and verb, with no change:
to act (verb), *an act* (noun); *to play* (verb), *a play* (noun).

Rule 128   The present participle form of the verb is often used as an adjective

Sometimes the adjective ending in **ing** goes in front of the noun in the usual way:
I watched the drifting clouds, and listened to the singing birds, and paddled in the babbling brook. The steady
drizzling rain went on unending. She dealt him a stinging blow on the cheek. The rising moon lit up the scene.

However, this sort of adjective very often goes after its noun - which is most unusual in English.
This order of words is nearly always used when the adjective ending in **ing** is linked to some
additional description:
The shape lurking in the shadows gave a low growl. Have you noticed anyone using the copier ?
They heard the engine throbbing under the deck beneath their feet. There is a man waiting for you.

Sometimes it is not clear whether the additional description is linked to the ING-word or not; then the order
of the words is a matter of choice: *I watched the drifting clouds in the the sky* is not so good *as I watched the*
clouds drifting in the sky, because there does seem to be a clear link.
She dealt him a blow stinging on the cheek would be wrong; it is simply not normal English use.

On the other hand: *I saw the moon rising* and *I saw the rising moon* are both correct, but have slightly
different meanings. There is no absolute rule about this. If in doubt put the an adjective in **ing** in front of
its noun - unless the adjective is linked to another group of words, in which case put it and the words with it
together after the noun.

When a description of this sort using a participle is not essential to the rest of the sentence, but merely adds some
interest, we often separate it off by using commas before and after.
This is a particularly good idea if the description is a long one:
The count, rising to his feet with a malicious smile and stroking his moustache, moved in for the kill.
Make sure you use both commas - beginning and end - and not just one of them.

Sometimes a phrase of this sort can go first, before the noun (or pronoun) it describes has been mentioned:
Wanting to attract the president's attention, I waved my hand in the air, forgetting I was holding Billy's toy gun.
The first phrase (*wanting to attract the president's attention*) describes *I*, even though it comes before it. The last phrase (*forgetting I was holding Billy's toy gun*) also describes, or adds to, the pronoun *I*. Where there are two adjectival phrases involving participles like this, it is quite usual to put one before and one after.

Make sure your adjective phrase is attached to the right noun or pronoun:
Walking along the beach, the cliffs can now be seen is very odd, since the cliffs should really keep still. Yet in this sentence the only noun that *walking* could possibly describe is *cliffs*. In this case what is needed is something like:
As you walk along the beach you can see the cliffs.

There is also something called an **absolute** construction, when a noun or pronoun plus a describing participle is separated off from the rest of the sentence. Here are two examples:
That being acceptable to all concerned, we shall proceed to the next point.
The committee having been duly elected, the House adjourned.
The first of these means: *Since that is acceptable to all concerned, we shall proceed to the next point.*
The second means: *When it had duly elected the committee, the House (i.e. the House of Commons) adjourned.*
You need to be able to understand writing that uses the absolute construction; in your own writing you can probably manage without it.

Rule 129   The past participle form of the verb is often used as an adjective

The form of the verb which you have already learnt as the past participle is very often used as an adjective. This form commonly ends in ED, but some verbs have irregular past participles, and it would be sensible to check back with *Rules 63* and *66* to *70* about the formation of past participles.

These verbal adjectives (often ending in *ed*) can go in front of their noun in the normal way, but the same rule applies to them as to the similar adjectives ending in *ing*.
When they are linked to another group of words, they normally follow their noun.

You will see how this works from these examples:
Young Johnson is a ruined man. Yes indeed, he is a man ruined by strong drink.
Let the chosen one come forward. This is the child chosen by the congregation.
The beaten team were even jeered by their own supporters. Any team beaten ten - nil needs a new goalkeeper.

Rule 130   The infinitive may also be used like an adjective

The use of the **infinitive** as an **adjective** is much less common.
The infinitive (with *to*) when used this way always follows its noun:
*He is the man **to see**. The only thing **to do** is apologise. Do you know the correct way **to use** an infinitive ?*

The infinitive used like this as an adjective generally implies some sort of advice or obligation.

Rule 131 Adverbs are generally formed from adjectives

Adverbs are generally formed from adjectives: add **LY** to the adjective to form the adverb:
soft - softly, bad - badly, fortunate - fortunately, wise - wisely, silent - silently, audacious - audaciously.

If the adjective already ends in **l**, then the adverb will end in **lly**.
If the adjective already ends in **ll**, then simply add **y**
to form the adverb. For example: *thoughtful - thoughtfully, dull - dully.*
Do not try to use **lly** as if it were the normal adverb ending.

Most adjectives ending in **e** form their adverbs in the normal way except: *true - truly; due - duly, undue - unduly.*
If an adjective ends in **le**, remove the e and add **y** (not **ly**): *able - ably, visible - visibly, noble - nobly.*

If an adjective ends in **y**, then change the **y** to **i** and add **ly** to form the adverb:
merry - merrily, happy - happily, busy - busily, dry - drily (though *dryly* also exists).
But notice the exceptions: *wry - wryly* and *sly - slyly.*

There are some **adjectives** which already end in **ly**. Some of them can form adverbs by changing the y to i and adding **ly**: silly - sillily. Some use the same form for adjective and adverb: *kindly* (adjective - but can be used as an adverb without change). Some are (almost) never used in an adverbial form: *ugly* (adjective only).
It is best to find an alternative word to use in difficult cases.

The **verbal adjectives** in **ing** sometimes have adverbs formed from them: *willingly, laughingly, sportingly.*
However, you should be careful as many such theoretically possible adverbs would not make sense, and so in practice do not exist.
In some cases there is an alternative adjective available: *hopingly* does not exist because *hopefully* does its job.

Rule 132 Some adverbs do not end in LY

Examples of common adverbs which do not add **ly** are: *fast, hard, much, well, late, soon, far, enough.*

Of these, *fast, hard, much, far* and *late* are all the same as the corresponding adjectives:
You haven't eaten much (adjective) *meat. No, I don't like it much* (adverb).
They travelled far (adverb) *to a far* (adjective) *country.*
He ran fast (adverb) *in a fast* (adjective) *race.*
A late (adjective) *connection meant that we did not arrive late* (adverb) *after all.*
The exercise is hard (adjective), *but you must work hard* (adverb) *at it.*
Notice that *hard* has a rather different meaning in its two uses here.

Also notice that there are adverbs *hardly* and *lately*, but they have special meanings.
Hardly means *with difficulty*: *I could hardly do* (I almost could not do) *such a hard exercise.*
Lately means *in recent time*: *He has been working late* (to a late hour) *at the office lately* (recently).

Well is the adverb from **good**: *You have behaved well* (adverb); *you are a good* (adjective) *girl.*

There are also some adverbs that do not have any corresponding adjectives: *very, never, almost, also, too, seldom, often, always, already, then, now, only* (though this is really an adverb from *one*).

Notice the adverbs formed from numbers: *once, twice* (and *thrice*, which is now not much used).

Rule 133   Adverbs are used to modify verbs

An adverb will tell you more about the action of a verb. It can be said to describe a verb in the way that an adjective describes a noun. Most commonly it tells you how (or in what manner) the action was carried out. However, it may also tell you when, where and why the action happens.

Here are some examples of the different sorts of adverbs:
Adverbs of **manner** (the most common) tell you **how**:
slowly, wickedly, intently, greedily, fast, happily, hard.
Adverbs of **degree** tell you **how much**:
almost, even, rather, very, too, much, more, only, also, most.
Adverbs of **place** tell you **where**:
here, there, nowhere, somewhere, anywhere, everywhere, inside, outside.
Adverbs of **number** tell you **how often**:
once, twice, seldom, always, ever, never, often, frequently, generally.
Adverbs of **time** tell you **when**:
before, already, soon, then, now, ago, once.
You may have noticed that adverbs of time and number may well overlap. These different categories are only to show you the large number of jobs adverbs have to do in modifying verbs; they are not something you need to learn.

You should have noticed, however, that it is the adverbs of manner (*how* adverbs) that are generally formed in the usual way from adjectives, and the other sorts of adverbs that have their own form. It is these other adverbs that you need to be careful with - particularly as some of the same words may not always be adverbs. This is not surprising. The part of speech a particular word is depends on the job it is doing in the sentence.

Yes, no and *not* are adverbs.
Several of the question words are also adverbs: *how, when, where, why* (but **not** *who, which, what*).

Rule 134   Adverbs may be used in conjunction with other adverbs

You should not be surprised that two adverbs can be used together. It is after all very common for two or more adjectives to be used together.
Sometimes when two adverbs are used together, they each separately modify or add to the meaning of the verb:
Slowly and *silently the monster approached.*(Two adverbs of manner, telling you how.)
Afterwards the crowd swiftly dispersed. (Firstly an adverb telling you when, then one telling you how.)
There, faintly I could already see the ship. (*There* is an adverb of place; *faintly* is an adverb of manner; *already* is an adverb of time.)

On other occasions two adverbs are used together so that one modifies the other:
She has done the job quite well. (*Quite* qualifies *well*, reducing its effect.)
There has almost never been a similar situation. (*Almost* limits *never*.)
You're driving very carefully today. (*Very* gives additional force to *carefully*, but does not affect *today*.)
When an adverb is used to modify another adverb, it is placed immediately in front of the adverb it affects, with the exception of *not*, which nearly always stays with the verb: *You're not driving very carefully today.*
In this example, **not very carefully** all really belong together; but, although *very* is in front of the adverb it modifies (*carefully*), *not* keeps its usual place in the middle of the verb.

Rule 135   Adverbs may be used to modify adjectives

In fact you already know of one way in which this happens. If you check back to *Rule 46* you will see that the comparative and superlative of longer adjectives are formed by attaching *more* and *most* to them:
beautiful - more beautiful - most beautiful;   unusual - more unusual - most unusual.

In all these cases the words *more* and *most* are in fact adverbs.
What they are doing is modifying the meaning of the adjective - making it stronger.

Other adverbs can also modify adjectives in various ways.
This particularly applies to adverbs of degree and most especially to the adverbs **very** and **too**:
Jimmy is a very naughty boy. This track is too dangerous for me. He employed some carefully chosen words.
I was very nearly late for work. (Notice the two adverbs (*very* and *nearly*) modifying the adjective.)
He was really too young to volunteer. You are much too careless with your grammar.
That is a very badly written exercise. He is almost fifteen.

Try to **avoid** using *really* as a substitute for *very* as in expressions like: *That was really nice.*

Rule 136   Most adverbs have comparative and superlative forms

Adverbs that end in **ly** form their **comparative** and **superlative** using **more** and **most**, in the same way as longer adjectives, as you have already seen in *Rule 46*.

Here are some examples of the comparative and superlative forms of adverbs:
slowly - more slowly - most slowly; happily - more happily - most happily;
unfortunately - more unfortunately - most unfortunately.

Adverbs that have the **same form as** their **adjectives**, have the **same comparative and superlative**:
fast (adverb and adjective) - *faster* (adverb and adjective) - *fastest* (adverb and adjective).

Better and **best** are the comparative and superlative of the adjective **good** and also of the adverb **well**.

Adverbs of manner can form comparatives and superlatives in one of the two ways just described.
Other adverbs, particularly those that do **not** end in **ly**, and do not have any corresponding adjective, tend
to have **no comparative and superlative forms.**

This is often as you would expect, since their meaning makes such forms impossible. It would not make sense
to talk of 'more never' or 'most always'.
However, *more often* and *most often* do exist - again as you would expect, since they clearly do make sense.

Other adverbs can be used to **modify** further **the comparative** and (rather more uncommonly) superlative forms:
marginally quicker than before; slightly farther on; certainly the most serious accident

Rule 137 Adverbs should be placed close to the word they modify

This is a very general rule, since in practice adverbs can go in most places in a sentence, when they are being used to modify a verb. The three commonest places are at the beginning of the sentence; at the end of the sentence; and close to the main verb (before or after) or in the middle of a compound verb.

Look at these examples:
(i) ***Frequently*** *we went to see Mrs Smith.*   *(ii)* *We went to see Mrs Smith* ***frequently***.
(iii) *We* ***frequently*** *went to see Mrs Smith.*   *(iv)* *We went* ***frequently*** *to see Mrs Smith.*

In the first of these, since the **adverb** comes **first** in the sentence, it is given particular importance.
The second and third examples show the commonest place for the adverb.
In short sentences (especially those with just a subject and verb) the **adverb** very frequently goes **at the end**, as in the second example; and you are unlikely to be wrong if you put it there.
In very many sentences the **adverb** can also be placed immediately after the subject and **before the main verb**. This is its position in the third sentence above.
The fourth example above seems a little unusual, because the adverb splits the main verb from the following infinitive which is closely connected to it. However, it is still not incorrect.

In a sentence where there is a compound verb, the adverb often goes after the first auxiliary verb:
I have sometimes been there. You should certainly have seen it. It would never have survived.
Some adverbs seem to prefer this position:
almost, also, always, sometimes, just, ever, never, often, even, hardly, nearly, still for example.

There are two places in the sentence: *We went to see Mr Smith* where the adverb should **not** go:
(a) **Between the verb and its object**, or even between the verb and any part of the sentence which follows it.
We went to see frequently Mrs Smith is wrong; so are: *I want to see now you; and we chose yesterday the new candidate, they go often for a drive, and he lost completely his temper.*
(b) **Splitting the infinitive.** The infinitive is: *to see.* '*We went to frequently see Mrs Smith*' would be wrong.
The main reason it is incorrect is that *frequently* is now linked to the wrong verb. It belongs with *went*, not with *see*.
Keep adverbs close to the verb they are modifying, especially is there is a possibility of confusion.
There is also a general objection to splitting infinitives. It is no longer wrong in spoken or even in most written English. However, avoid doing it in exams and formal English. Certainly do not split infinitives with long phrases. *To boldly go* may be acceptable; *to finally and with enormous difficulty succeed* is not.

The **question words**, of course, go at the **beginning** of the question: *Where are you going ?*
Other adverbs in questions generally go **at the end**: *Are you ready yet ? Will you come quietly ?*
However, those adverbs which prefer a position in the middle, stay in the middle in questions:
Will she ever be ready ? Is she nearly ready ? Do you always go to Majorca ? Could I just have a cup of tea ?
But notice: *Do you come here often ?* which is as good English as: *Do you often come here ?*

In **commands** the **adverb** usually goes **at the end** of the sentence:
Meet me tomorrow. Write to me regularly. Show me immediately. Please do not go yet.
However, it can sometimes go first: *Now stop it ! Quickly, pull over !*

When an adverb is **modifying another adverb or an adjective**, it normally goes **directly in front** of the adverb or adjective it is modifying: *nearly new, often undecided, terribly painful, fairly unexpected, slightly later.*
When there is a **list** of adjectives, put the adverb with the right one: *He was a tall, thin, slightly balding man.*
There are **exceptions**: *yours sincerely, yours faithfully* etc. at the end of letters are common examples.
Also, the adverb *enough* follows the adverb or adjective it modifies: *long enough, well enough* etc.

Rule 138   The passive is formed with the verb TO BE and the past participle

All tenses of the verb, and verb forms using other auxiliaries or modal verbs may have a passive form.
The passive is when the action of the verb returns to the subject, and is explained in *Rule 139*.

The **present passive** uses the **present tense** of the verb **to be** (*am, are, is*) **plus the past participle** of the verb.
The **future passive** uses the **future** tense of the verb **to be** (*shall be/will be*) plus the **past participle**.
The **past passive** uses the **past** tense of the verb **to be** (*was/were*) plus the **past participle**.
The **perfect passive** uses the **perfect** tense of the verb **to be** (*have been/has been*) plus the **past participle**.
The **pluperfect passive** uses the **pluperfect** of the verb **to be** (*had been*) plus the **past participle**.

Here are the main passive forms of the verb *to like*:

Present: *I am liked, you are liked, he/she/it is liked, we are liked, you are liked, they are liked*

Future: *I shall be liked, you will be liked, he/she/it will be liked, we shall be liked,*
you will be liked, they will be liked

Past: *I was liked, you were liked, he/she/it was liked, we were liked you were liked, they were liked*

Perfect: *I have been liked, you have been liked, he/she/it has been liked, we have been liked,*
you have been liked, they have been liked

Pluperfect: *I had been liked, you had been liked, he/she/it had been liked, we had been liked,*
you had been liked, they had been liked

Future Perfect: *I shall have been liked, you will have been liked, he/she/it will have been liked,*
we shall have been liked, you will have been liked, they will have been liked.

There are also **continuous** forms of the tenses. Of these the present and past are quite common and must be learnt:

Present: *I am being liked etc.*   **Past:** *I was being liked etc.*

The future, perfect, pluperfect and future perfect continuous are cumbersome, and not found or used very often.

Perfect: *I have been being liked* etc. Pluperfect: *I had been being liked* etc.
Future: *I shall be being liked* etc.   Future Perfect: *I shall have been being liked* etc

Here are examples of forms using other auxiliary verbs:
I can be liked, I could be liked, I would be liked, I should be liked,
I may be liked, I might be liked, I must be liked
I used to be liked, I am going to be liked
I ought to be liked, I have to be liked, I want to be liked
You can work out the other persons of the verb from the *I* form (the first person singular) that is given.
Remember that *modal* verbs do not change form.

Rule 139   The passive is used to indicate that the action returns to the subject

The **passive** is used when the **action** of the verb **is suffered** or experienced **by the subject**.
This is easiest to see when we compare the ordinary (or active) use of the verb and the passive:

Active: *The man is eating a fish.*   Passive: *The man is being eaten by a fish.*
Active: *I saw the hideous ghoul.*   Passive: *I was seen by the hideous ghoul.*
Active: *We have selected Miss Jones.*   Passive: *Miss Jones has been selected by us.*
Active: *Can Dawes arrange it ?*   Passive: *Can it be arranged by Dawes ?*
Active: *Janice had not seen Susan.*   Passive: *Susan had not been seen by Janice.*

When an adverb is used with a verb in the passive it may go at the end (*That horse is being ridden **fast**.*);
or after the first auxiliary (*We have **never** been invaded by our enemies.*); or directly in front of the main verb,
in its form as the past participle (*The fire was being **swiftly** extinguished.*).

In negative sentences the **not** goes immediately after the first auxiliary: *The rhino was not shot by the hunters.*
In questions, the subject and first auxiliary verb are reversed, in the usual way: *Has the house been demolished ?*
In commands, the form is **do not be**: *Do not be seen. Do not be captured.*

There is no direct passive form of tenses using *do* and *did*. You should use the equivalent form with the verb *to be*:
Active: *Did Robinson kill Tom ?*   Passive: *Was Tom killed by Robinson ?*

Intransitive verbs (verbs that do not take an object) have **no passive** form.

Rule 140   There are passive infinitives, participles and verbal nouns

The passive infinitives are formed, like the passive tenses, using the verb *to be*.
The ordinary (present) infinitive passive is formed with **to be** plus the **past participle**:
Active infinitive: *to like*   **passive infinitive:** *to be liked*

There is also a past (or perfect) passive infinitive, formed with **to have been** plus the **past participle**:
Perfect active infinitive: *to have liked*   **perfect passive infinitive:** *to have been liked*

These infinitives are used for much the same purposes as the active infinitives:
He wants nothing more than to be liked. I am not prepared to be swindled by the likes of you.
Do you want to be punished, boy ?   He is thought to have been killed with a blunt instrument.

Similarly there are passive participles and verbal nouns, formed with **being** plus the **past participle**:
Active participle/verbal noun: *liking*   **passive participle/verbal noun:** *being liked*
The past form of the verbal noun is formed with **having been** plus the **past participle**:
Active perfect participle/verbal noun: *having liked*   **passive past participle/verbal noun:** *having been liked*.

The use of these passive forms as verbal nouns is not specially difficult:
That fellow likes being liked.   I was trying to avoid being chosen.   Being beaten is most unpleasant.
He is furious at having been ignored by the committee. The decision having been made, we all went home.
Look at *Rule 128* for the special use of *having been liked* etc. as an adjective in absolute phrases.

A **future passive participle** can be formed with **going to be** *plus* the past participle: *going to be liked*.

68

Rule 141   The agent and instrument may be stated with a passive verb

Many of the examples of the passive in *Rules 139* and *140* have an *agent*. You will remember that in a passive verb the action returns to the subject. The **agent** is the person or thing **responsible for the action**: the one who did it.

The **agent** is indicated by the word **by**, and usually follows directly after the passive verb:
*He was murdered **by** his brother.   We were directed here **by** the guide.   Mrs Wood is wanted **by** the police.*
*The film was watched **by** the whole school.   Hodge will be replaced **by** Sawyer.   He has been chosen **by** the party.*

There is no necessity to include an agent after a passive verb. In fact the passive is often used when the agent is not important (as explained in *Rule 142*).
Study these examples of passives without any stated agent:
Mrs Blenkinsop has been run over. (It does not matter at this stage whether it was by a bus or a car or a mule train.)
The explosion could be seen for miles. (The agent is 'anyone who was looking' - and clearly not important.)
Has your homework been collected yet ? (The collection is important, not who does it.)

Agents are often people, or abstract nouns that stand for people: *He was dismissed by London Transport.*
However, agents can sometimes be things, if those things can be said to act by themselves, without the intervention of another (human) agent.
The examples may help you to understand how this works:
*The city was destroyed **by fire**. He was tortured **by doubts**.*
*She was run over **by a bus** and killed immediately **by the force** of the impact.*

Do not confuse the agent with the *instrument*. The **instrument** is the **thing** used by the agent to carry out the action. The instrument may well be mentioned with active as well as passive verbs. The agent is not of course - because he or she or it is already there in the subject.
The instrument is generally indicated by the word **with**.

Look at these examples with agents and instruments:
*Mrs Plantagenet killed him **with an axe**.* (Active: the subject performs the action; the instrument is mentioned.)
*He was killed **with an axe by Mrs Plantagenet**.* (Passive: the action comes back to the subject, and both agent and instrument are included.)
*The two presidents signed the agreement **with a golden pen*** (active - instrument only), or alternatively:
*The agreement was signed **with a golden pen by the two presidents*** (passive - agent and instrument).
*This window has been cut **with a diamond*** (passive - instrument mentioned, but no agent).

In this last example the active version: *A diamond has cut this window* seems a bit odd, because diamonds do not do things by themselves. We would be happier with: *Someone has cut this window **with** a diamond* (or *used a diamond to cut this window.*)
This is better because instruments (as distinct from agents) are not natural subjects of the verb.

Notice also the different uses of *by*, *with*, *of*, and *from* in describing how things are made:
It is made of stone means stone is the only substance or main substance it contains.
It is made from stone tells us the original material before construction started.
It is made with stone suggests that, though stone is used, there are other things involved too.
It was made with stone tools tells us the instrument used to make it.
It was made by Stone tells us that Mr Stone carried out the manufacture....

Rule 142   The passive is preferred to the active when the agent is irrelevant

This means that we use a passive verb form, rather than an active one, when it does not really matter who performed the action. What matters is that the action was performed, or that it happened to a particular person. Sometimes the agent is people in general, or could be anyone. Sometimes it is a person or people who have already been mentioned, and do not need to be mentioned again. Look at the following examples, and explanations.

Gold has been discovered in Hampshire is better than *Someone has discovered gold in Hampshire.*
Herodotus is known as 'The Father of History' is much better than starting vaguely with: *People call Herodotus....*
Hundreds of people are killed every year on the roads is better than an active form not only because the agent is obviously a general one: 'people driving cars and lorries' but also because the people being killed are the important thing in the sentence.

This rule still applies when the agent is mentioned, but is not the most important part of the information. So we would say: *The Prime Minister has been assassinated by terrorists* (passive) rather than: *Terrorists have assassinated the Prime Minister* (active).

Notice that the passive is also often used with verbs introduced by **it**: *It is forbidden to walk on the grass.* Check back to *Rule 97* for details of this.
Rather similar are instructions like: *Shoes must be removed before entering the mosque.*

Rule 143   Reflexive verbs have the same subject and object

In a verb in the passive, the action returns to the subject.
When a verb is used reflexively, it is followed by a pronoun that stands for the same person as the subject.

The **reflexive pronouns** are forms of the personal pronouns (which you already know):
myself, yourself, himself, herself, itself, ourselves, yourselves, themselves.

Here are some examples of reflexive verbs:
Matthew shot himself in the foot. I could not trust myself. We have only ourselves to blame.
Let yourself go! Do you want to hurt yourselves ? She has excelled herself.
Notice that the reflexive pronouns do have two *you* forms, one for singular and one for plural.

There are also other uses of reflexive pronouns.They may be used to emphasize the person performing the action:
I did it myself. ('It was done by me, personally, and not by anyone else.')
We ourselves are to blame. ('We are to blame, and no-one else.')
In the second example it would be wrong to put *ourselves* at the end, because it would look as if it was the object of the verb - which would make the meaning of the sentence slightly different. In the first example it can go at the end, because there is clearly an object already there.

The forms **by myself, by yourself** (and sometimes **all by myself**) etc. are sometimes used in this way, to emphasize the subject: *Little Jimmy drew this picture all by himself.*
However, these forms also have the similar, but slightly different meaning of **alone** as in:
The woodcutter lived by himself in the forest.

Exercise 44
Insert one of the following modal verb forms in each sentence. You may use each form only once:
would wouldn't might should may can must may could couldn't.

(1) I .... have sworn I saw him there.
(2) .... you like another cup ?
(3) I ....do that if I was you.
(4) Jackie .... have written to her sister.
(5) He .... come if he's free.
(6) Mrs Bulstrode ....wait any longer.
(7) You boys ....be in room six.
(8) They .... have left before we arrived.
(9) She says she .... swim twelve lengths.
(10) Please .... I leave the room ?

Exercise 45
In these sentences insert the correct word from the choice given you:
(1) You can/may almost see the top from here.   (2) They must/should have been here by now.
(3) After the noise had died down, we can/could hear the distant wailing of the siren.
(4) They may/should possibly be in the top drawer.(5) Could/would you mind waiting for a moment.
(6) I wouldn't/couldn't be seen dead wearing that.   (7) She must/might have been mad to believe him.
(8) If you must/should know, I could/may have come to the party, but I decided not to.
(9) You could/must have knocked me down with a feather after that.

Exercise 46
Correct the mistake made in using the auxiliary/modal verb in each of these sentences:
(1) When we were going up the hill Mr Pooter can not keep up with the rest of us.
(2) May you stop that noise, please.   (3) She could just about to manage another ice-cream.
(4) We may not go through that door because it is always kept locked.
(5) We cannot go through that door because it is strictly forbidden.
(6) By the look on your face the interview should have been very unpleasant.
(7) I will probably be going to Ruth's this afternoon; shall you be coming with me ?
(8) Will you mind walking this way, madam.   (9) I can't walk that way if I tried.
(10) Would you play that awful drum while mummy's trying to read, darling ?

Exercise 47
Correct the mistakes in these sentences:
(1) It would be wrong to raising taxes again.
(2) She had always wanted writing a book
(3) I am sick of their chattering's noise.
(4) I find the learning Urdu difficult.
(5) Do you know to drive a car ?
(6) I admire the choir singing.
(7) We sent them a demanding letter all the money they still owe us.
(8) Looking out of our window, the Seven Sisters can be clearly seen.
(9) She gave the sleeping baby a kiss loving on the forehead.
(10) Father Robin is the chosen man to be the new bishop.

Exercise 48
Form nouns from these verbs:

(1) choose	(2) elect	(3) decide	(4) arrange	(5) inform
(6) cut	(7) create	(8) conquer	(9) give	(10) shoot
(11) allow	(12) lose	(13) seize	(14) prove	(15) move
(16) carry	(17) deceive	(18) determine	(19) bless	(20) permit

Exercise 49

(a) Form adverbs from these adjectives:
(1) ready   (2) fearful   (3) full   (4) horrible   (5) sly

(b) Now give the comparative and superlative forms of the same five adverbs.

Exercise 50

(1) Give the adverb formed from *good*, together with its comparative and superlative.
(2) Write a sentence of your own in which you use the same word as adjective and as adverb.
(3) Write two sentences, one using *hard* and the other using *hardly*, with their correct meanings.
(4) Give two examples of each category of adverb: (a) manner, (b) degree, (c) place, (d) number, (e) time. Try to think of examples of your own, rather than ones mentioned in the book.
(5) Write a sentence in which you use an adverb to modify another adverb.
(6) Write a sentence in which you use an adverb to modify an adjective.
(7) Write a sentence in which you use two adverbs in different positions to modify the same verb.

Exercise 51

(a) Change these sentences from active to passive, keeping the same meaning.
(1) Billy is speaking to the headmaster.   (2) Our forces had attacked the enemy.
(3) Moriarty killed him with an axe, Watson.   (4) Those girls have been chasing the boys again.
(5) Did any of you see Mrs Lightfinger opening the office safe this morning ?

(b) Now repeat the exercise, this time reversing the meaning of the sentences in your version in the passive.
Clue: The original subject should be the subject again.

Exercise 52

(a) Change these sentences from passive to active, keeping the same meaning.
(1) Mark has been eaten by a huge fish.
(2) In a moment I had been seized by the squirming tentacle of a giant octopus.
(3) Cloggs was warned about his tackling by the referee.
(4) He will never again be selected by the committee for a position of responsibility.
(5) This victory has been delivered by our generals despite their previous incompetence.

(b) Now repeat the exercise, once again reversing the meaning of the sentences in the passive.
The same clue applies as in the previous exercise.

Exercise 53

(1) Write a sentence of your own using a passive verb with agent but not instrument stated.
(2) Write a similar sentence, this time stating instrument but not agent.
(3) Write a similar sentence stating both agent and instrument.
(4) Write a similar sentence where the stated agent is an abstract noun.
(5) Write a similar sentence where agent (and instrument) are left out because they are irrelevant.

Rule 144   Personal pronouns change their form when they are the object

You already recognize the personal pronouns when they are used as the subject of the verb:
I, you (singular and plural), *he, she, it, we, they.*

You also know their use in the object form, though you may not always have recognized that is what they are.
The object forms have been briefly mentioned earlier in *Rule 90*, but are explained more fully here.
The personal pronouns are very frequently used as the object of the verb (the one who receives the action).

The correct forms of the personal pronouns when they are the **object** of the verb are as follows:

I	becomes	**me**	**We**	becomes	**us**			
He	becomes	**him**	**She**	becomes	**her**	**They**	becomes	**them**

You and It stay the same.

Look at these examples: *He* (subject) *was annoying* **me** (object), *and* **I** (subject) *was annoying* **him** (object).
We (subject) *have always liked* **her** (object), *but* **she** (subject) *has never liked* **us** (object).
If that dog bites **me**, *I shall bite* **it** *back.   The police pursued* **them** *onto the roof before* **they** *gave up.*

The **object form** of the personal pronouns is also used **after prepositions**:
Were you looking **for me** *? Give it* **to him**. *There were hundreds* **of them**.

Notice also that it is normal in spoken English to say: *It is me, It was him* etc.
In written English, strictly speaking, the correct forms are: *It is I, It was he* etc.
However, the correct forms now sound very odd, as they are almost never used in the spoken language,
or in dialogue when you are writing. So the spoken forms are no longer very wrong, even in formal
written English.

Rule 145   The personal pronouns have possessive forms

Once again you are familiar with these forms, but probably had not realised what they were:

I becomes mine in the possessive
You becomes yours in the possessive
He becomes his in the possessive
She becomes hers in the possessive
It becomes its in the possessive
We becomes ours in the possessive
They becomes theirs in the possessive.

These words are pronouns, and should be used by themselves, and not with a noun:
Those books are mine. She claims that they are hers. Theirs is the third house from the end.
Which one is yours ? Can you see which is ours ? It isn't his.

Read the following rule carefully for some more notes about the use of these pronouns.

Rule 146   There are possessive pronouns and possessive adjectives

A **pronoun** stands in for a noun and so is used **by itself**.
An **adjective** generally goes **with a noun**, or as a **complement** after the verb *to be*.
The personal possessive pronouns and personal possessive adjectives are slightly different in some cases:

Adjective: **my**   -   *That is my dog. They are my sisters. My writing is not very good. Have you seen my book ?*
Pronoun: **mine**   -   *That is mine. Mine is the biggest one. Where is mine ? Mine isn't very good.*

Adjective: **your**   -   *It's all your fault. Your writing is worse than mine. Is that your bike ? Your sister is pretty.*
Pronoun: **yours**   -   *It's yours if you want it. Yours is over there. Have you got yours yet ?*

Adjective and pronoun: **his** - *That's his (pronoun). No, his (pronoun) is over there.*
                                    Is it his (pronoun) ? Yes, it is his (adjective) dog.

Adjective: **her**   -   *Her house is near ours. Have you seen her room. She wants her pen back.*
Pronoun: **hers**   -   *That's not hers; hers is over there. I don't think it is hers. Hers is the best.*

Adjective: **its**   -   *Is that its kennel ? Yes, the aardvark loves its old kennel.*
In theory *its* could also exist as a possessive pronoun, but is very rarely used in that way.

Adjective: **our**   -   *Our side will win. Have you got our tickets ?   We want our money back.*
Pronoun: **ours**   -   *Ours is the best. No it's not; ours is. He wants to know if we would like ours now.*

Adjective: **their**   -   *Their loss is our gain. What did you think of their performance ?*
Pronoun: **theirs**   -   *Theirs is going to win. Which one is theirs ? I didn't like theirs.*

Do not mix up **its** (meaning *of it*) and **it's** (meaning *it is*).
Do not mix up **their** (meaning *of them*) and **there** (as in *there is*) or **they're** (meaning *they are*).
Do not mix up **theirs** (meaning *of them* - pronoun) and **there's** (meaning *there is*).

Rule 147   The personal pronouns have some special uses

We have already seen that **it** is used as a **general subject** of the verb (*Rule 97)*, as in:
It is fine today. It's very late. It will be fish for dinner again. It's a long way to Tipperary.
The pronoun **it** also sometimes appears as a **general object**: *I won't stand for it any longer.*

We also use **they** as a **general subject** meaning *people in general* (especially in the use of *they say*):
They say it's going to be another cold winter.
A similar use of *they* means something like *people in power*:
They're increasing taxes again. They should do something about it.

You is sometimes used as a **general subject** to mean *people in general* as well:
You can't walk down the street after dark these days. You can get away with murder if you know the right people.
You aren't allowed to talk after lights out. You don't want to go in there! You'd never believe it.
You appears as a **general object** too in: *Well, I ask you!* (meaning something like: *Everyone agrees, don't they ?*)

Rule 148   The personal pronouns may be used together with one other

The use of two personal pronouns together only causes confusion because of the following general rule:
When using a noun or another personal pronoun together with **I** : **I** *goes second*.
So: *John and I went to the park. You and I can manage it together. Mrs Goodbody, he and I were in the queue.*

The **other personal pronouns** used with a noun often go **first**:
You and David can go first. She and Dr Cuticle have both seen him.

Because we are so used to *you and I*, *he and I* etc. we sometimes use them when we should not:
The manager wants to see him and me (**not** *he and I*, because the two pronouns are the **object**, not the subject).
It will be up to you and me (**not** *you and I*, because the pronouns follow a preposition, so, once again, they have to be in the object form).

So long as you remember that **I** is used for the **subject**, you should not make this mistake.

When there are two pronouns together, or a pronoun used with a noun, as the subject of the verb, there can sometimes be some doubt as to what form of the verb to use.
The first thing to remember is that if there are **two pronouns**, or a **noun and a pronoun**, then there are two people, so the verb is going to be **plural**.
That is all the information you need in nearly every case:
You and Mrs Ponsonby are (not *is*) *going to the theatre. Smith and I were* (not *was*) *fighting.*
You and he have (not *has*) *won. She and Brenda dislike* (not *dislikes*) *Mr Smidgeon.*

The only problem which might arise is in deciding between *shall* and *will* in the future tense. If **I** is one of the pronouns in a plural subject, you can use *shall* (but even then *will* is not really wrong). In all other cases, use *will*.

Rule 149   ONE and other numbers may be used as pronoun or adjective

You know how to use *one* as an adjective, when it simply means ***the number one***:
One boy is to come with me, the rest are to wait here. I want one apple and two oranges, please.

Notice that with **book, chapter, page** and **number**, *one* and the other **numbers** go **second**:
Turn to page one. Read chapter five in Book Two. What have you put for number seven ?

One and the other **numbers** are often used **by themselves** (which means effectively used as pronouns) and are often followed by *of* plus a noun:
One of our ships is missing. He's one of them. Eleven of us set off, but only one of the party returned.

Notice that ***one or two*** means *a few*, or any small number.

One is also used as a pronoun to indicate one particular item out of several already mentioned:
I'd like the smallest one please. He's the one who did it. Can I have that one over there ?
Notice that ***one*** can have a **plural** (*ones*) in this use:
Which ones would you like, madam ? These ones are particularly tasty.

One is used as a pronoun in various phrases, some of which are set out here.

One is used in contrast to **the other** when comparing two things:
One was red, the other was blue. You can't tell one from the other.
One is used in contrast to **others** when comparing more than two things:
This one is very ancient, the others are fakes.

One another is used in the same way as **each other** to show shared action or feelings:
They dislike one another intensely.   They don't even speak to each other.

For one thing means one reason (out of many) is being given:
What's wrong with her ? Well, for one thing she's a snob.

One day, one morning etc. mean on a given day - but exactly when does not matter:
It all began one summer's day in 1965. One day you'll regret this.

Once upon a time, used at the start of fairy stories, is rather similar, but is only used when starting fairy stories.

One is also used as a general personal pronoun of the third person (with possessive and reflexive forms as well):
One would prefer a better seat. They provide one with adequate accommodation.
One does not expect to have one's word questioned. One must do things for oneself.
This use is now regarded as rather 'posh'. Unless you are prime minister or a member of the royal family, use *you, I, they* or *we* instead.

Notice the **indefinite** (vague) forms of one: *someone* and *anyone* - and the identical *somebody* and *anybody*.
Someone is used in **positive** sentences; **anyone** in **negative** sentences, and some questions:
Is anyone there ? Somebody must be there. I can't see anybody. I saw someone over there.
These forms are used for people. For things use *something* and *anything* in exactly the same way.

Notice that *someone, somebody, something*, and *anyone, anybody, anything* should all be followed by a **singular** not a plural verb:
*Someone is coming (**not** are coming). Is anyone there (**not:** Are anyone there) ?*

As we have mentioned before, English does not like words being repeated unnecessarily.
One way in which this is avoided is by using *one* and *ones*, *some* and *any* as pronouns, to indicate a noun that has already been used.

The following examples show how this is done:
He'd got a whole bag of sweets, but he didn't ask me if I wanted any.
He'd got a whole bag of sweets, but he wouldn't give me one.
Would you like a banana ? - I've got some lovely ones.

Rule 150   THIS, THAT, THESE and THOSE are used as adjectives or pronouns

This means **the one here**, or *the nearest*, or *the one in possession*, or sometimes (in time) *the one now*.
These is the *plural* of *this*.

That means **the one there**, or *the more distant*, or occasionally (in time) *the one then* or *the one in the past*.
or *the one not in possession*.
Those is the *plural* of *that*.

Remember the difference between an adjective and a pronoun:.
An adjective goes with a noun, a pronoun stands by itself.
The words *this*, *that*, *these* and *those* can be used either as adjectives or pronouns.

Here are examples of uses as pronouns:

This is the one I want. (Meaning *the one here* - used as the subject of the sentence.)
Do you want these ? (Meaning *the ones here* - object of a question.)

That's the man who did it. (Meaning *the one over there* - used as the subject of the sentence.)
Do you want one of those ? (Meaning *the ones over there* - used after a preposition.)

Here are some examples of the same words used as adjectives:

This book is boring. (Adjective describing *book* - meaning *the one here*.)
Do you want these cakes or not ? (Adjective describing cakes - meaning the ones being offered.)
I have never seen that man before in my life. (Adjective describing man - meaning the one over there.)
Have you looked at those books I told you to read ? (Adjective describing *books* - suggesting that the books are not present at the time, but have been mentioned in the past.)

In questions **that** is used for something *unknown*; **this** for something *known*:
Who's that ? (Meaning the same as*: Who's there ?*)   *What's that ?*
Who's this then ? What's all this, my lad ?

That is used as a pronoun rather more than *this*, and in many ways it means very little (rather like *it* or *there* as the subject of the verb, as explained in *Rules 96* and *97*).

Here are some particular uses of *that*:
That's a good boy and ***There's a good girl*** mean (if anything) something like:
If you do what I am suggesting you will be a good boy/girl, or: *I am pleased you are doing what I want.*
That's right means *yes*, while: ***That's alright*** is used as a vague agreement or an acknowledgement of thanks.
That's it means *You have got it right.* ***That's that*** means: *It is finished now.*
That will do and ***That's enough*** mean *Stop it!*
That will never do suggests that something is not acceptable.

There is another use of **that** in sentences like: *He's the one that did it*, which we shall look at later.

And there is another use of **that** in sentences like: *He said that he was going*, which we shall also look at later.

Rule 151   HERE and THERE are used in several special ways

The distinction between **here** and **there** is very similar to the distinction between *this* and *that*.

Here means *in this place*.
There means *in that place*.

However, these meanings are not always clear in some of their uses, as you can see from the examples.

Firstly you should check back to *Rule 96* for the use of **there** as the *subject of the verb TO BE*, in sentences like:
There is a tavern in the town.   There were three of us in the room.   There can be no mistake.

There and **here** both have their simple meanings in:
Have you ever been there ? We're nearly there. Come here! Wait over there. You can't go in here.

Notice that *over here* and *over there* mean much the same as *here* and *there*.

There and **here** do not have much meaning at all in expressions like:
Here you are. This is usually said when giving something to somebody.
There you are. This can also be said when giving something.
However, *there you are* is often used to claim that a point has been proved:
There you are! I said you'd got number six wrong.
For some reason *there you go*, which makes no sense at all, is now often used instead of *there you are*.

There is used by itself almost as an interjection, without meaning very much:
There! I told you it was in the cupboard.
There! There! is used to soothe or comfort children: *There, there! Never mind!*
You already know about: *There's a good boy* etc. from the last rule.

Here it is/Here they are. There it is/There they are.
Both these expressions are used to indicate that someone/something has arrived, been found etc:
Here it is, in the drawer. There they are, just getting off the bus.

Notice that we like to use **here** with *come*, and **there** with *go*.
When the subject of a sentence of this sort beginning with *here* or *there* is a noun, we reverse the normal order, and put verb before noun:
Here comes Susan now. There goes my train.
When the subject is one of the personal pronouns, we keep the usual order:
Here she comes. There it goes.

Here and there means *in many places*.
But when we say: *That is **neither here nor there***, we mean it is irrelevant.

There and then, or *then and there* mean *at that time and that place*, or just *immediately*.

Look here is used to call attention, often as a kind of protest: *Look here, you silly boy !*

Here goes means something like: *Look, I am about to start (something difficult).*

Rule 152 A phrase is a group of words without a verb

You are already familiar with very many phrases, though you may not have realised that is what they were.
An article, adjective and noun make up one sort of phrase (a noun phrase): *the clever girl, a difficult journey*.

A **noun phrase** is any sort of phrase which has a noun in it or does the job of a noun.
Here are two examples of noun phrases:
That boy, Thompson, has given the whole class German measles.   *That boy Thompson* is the subject of the
sentence; *the whole class* is the indirect object; *German measles* is the object. So there are three noun phrases,
each used to play a different part in the sentence.

Driving a heavy lorry through thick fog is not a very pleasant experience. The words *a very pleasant experience*
are one simple sort of noun phrase. The subject of the sentence, *driving a heavy lorry*, is also a noun phrase. The
noun in it is a verbal noun.
We could equally have used an infinitive to form the noun phrase: *To drive a heavy lorry.*
Check back to *Rules 123* to *126* for the use of verbal nouns ending in ING, and *Rules 121* and *122* for some uses
of the infinitive.

An **adjective phrase** is any group of words used like an adjective.
So adjective phrases are used to describe nouns:
That boy in the second form with the catapult has broken the window of the headmaster's study.
With the catapult tells you what sort of boy it is; so does *in the second form*; so these are adjective phrases
describing *boy*. *Of the headmaster's study* tells you more about which window it was, so it is also an adjective
phrase, describing the word *window*.

*The message, written on the back of a cloakroom ticket handed to me by the attendant, was in a code now being
deciphered by our organization.*
All the adjective phrases in this long sentence contain verbal adjectives. *Written on the back of a cloakroom ticket*
is a phrase describing *message. Handed to me by the attendant* is a phrase telling us more about the *cloakroom
ticket. Currently being deciphered by our organization* is a phrase (using a present passive participle) telling us
more about the *code.* Look back at *Rules 128 and 129* for the use of participles as verbal adjectives.

An **adverb phrase** tells us the way in which the action of the verb is carried out: ***how, when, where, why*** etc.,
exactly as an adverb does. Once again here are two examples using adverb phrases:
At the last moment, with a single bound the hero leapt away from the closing jaws and through the attic window.
With a single bound tells us how the action was done (adverb phrase of manner); *at the last moment* tells us when
it was done (adverb phrase of time); then we have the other two adverb phrases (*from the closing jaws; through the
attic window*) saying where the action happened (adverb phrases of place).

*After a moment's silence, without waiting for an answer, she turned, despite all attempted explanations, and made
her way, in obvious fury, towards the door.* Firstly we have the adverb phrase of time (*after a moment's angry
silence*). *Without waiting for an answer; despite all attempted explanations; and in obvious fury* all describe how
she turned (adverb phrases of manner). *Towards the door*, an adverb phrase of place, tells us where.

You do not need to learn the names of these different sorts of phrases, but it may be useful to know what they are.
In fact the important thing to notice is that very many of them (especially the adverb and adjective phrases) are
introduced by prepositions.
Several of the following rules deal with common phrases of this sort, and the prepositions used with them.

Rule 153   Prepositions are often used to indicate time

Most of the prepositions about time are very obvious: *before, after, during, while, until*:
See you after lunch. It happened before three o'clock. She disappeared while walking in the park.
During the speeches there was some heckling. This state of affairs continued until the last war.
Notice that each of these prepositions is followed by a noun or noun phrase.

Other prepositions used to indicate time may need a little more care.
At is used for *times by the clock*: *at three o'clock, at twenty to ten, at seven forty-five, at half past one.*
Also: *at noon, at midday, at midnight, at the weekend* (but also: *during the weekend*)
At is used for *mealtimes* and the names of some important festivals or *holidays*:
at lunch, at breakfast, at dinner time; at Christmas, at Easter, at Whitsun.
At is used for other *particular points* in time: *at the moment of decision, at this time of crisis*

On is used for any *particular day*, including the *days of the week* and some special days:
on Friday, on the 10th of June, on the thirteenth, on New Year's Day, on Diwali.
In or **during** can both be used for *months, seasons, years, decades, centuries* and longer periods:
in May, during summer, in the winter, in 1960, during the nineteenth century, in the Middle Ages.
Notice that the seasons may have a definite article, or no article.
We say *in the afternoon* and *in the morning*, unless we say which afternoon or morning, when we use *on*:
on Friday afternoon, on Saturday morning.
We also use *on* when the indefinite article is used: *It was on a wet afternoon. It must be on a Friday morning.*
But notice: *once a day, twice a week, three times a year* etc. with no preposition.
Something may be *in the future, in the past* and (sometimes) *in the present*; but *at present* means *now.*
In the meantime means: *in the period before something happens*;
For the time being, at the moment and *for now* mean: *now and for some time but not permanently.*

We say *by day*, or *during the day*, or *in the daytime*, and sometimes *in the day*.
We say *at night*, or *by night*, or *in the night*, or *during the night*, or *at night time*.
Notice the use of **this** and **next**. *This* means the *first one to arrive*; *next* means the *second one to arrive*:
This Wednesday (the first Wednesday to come); *next Thursday* (the second Thursday to come).
Thursday week means *next Thursday* (not the Thursday in *this week* the Thursday in *next week*).
This afternoon means *the present afternoon*, but we do not say 'next afternoon'; we say: *tomorrow afternoon.*
Phrases of this sort, with *this* and *next* in them, *do not have any preposition.*

By is used to set a *latest time* for something to happen: *Be there by noon. It should be finished by next May.*
Until is used to set a *finishing time*: *Stay until seven, then go home. I shall wait until their arrival.*
Till is used with exactly the *same meaning as until*: *He often works till ten or eleven o'clock at night.*
Since is used to set a *start time* when something began in the *past*: *We have been going there since last July.*
Notice that with *since* the main verb is nearly always in the *perfect tense.*
In is used to set a *start time* when something will begin in the *future*: *Meet me in half an hour.*
In (and also **within**) is also used to set a maximum *future limit*: *I expect them in three days.*
Sometimes the word *time* is put on the end of that sort of sentence: *I'll meet you in an hour's time.*

For is used for *length of time*:
They stayed for three weeks. I can only stay for a minute or two. He spoke for ages and ages.
We have known about this for some time. Notice we say: *Wait a minute* without any preposition.

Rule 154 Prepositions are often used to indicate place

The main thing you need to learn in this Rule is, once again, when to use particular prepositions.

In is used with most *geographical locations* -
continents, countries, counties, districts, regions, cities, towns, villages, and even streets:
*In Asia, in the U.S.A., in Hampshire, in the Punjab, in the Midlands, in the North West, in eastern Europe,
in Lahore, in Edinburgh, in Dijon, in Stow-on-the-Wold, in Station Road,* but also *on State Street.*
We also say*: in town, in the city, in the road,* and *in the street,* but *on the pavement.*

At and **In** are the main prepositions of place.
You can be: *in front, in the middle, at the side, at the top* or *on top,* and *at the back;
at home* or *in the house* (but *in the home* is sometimes used about household objects).
Also notice the various adverbs: *indoors* and *outdoors* (or *out of doors*), *inside* and *outside,* or simply *in* or *out.*
So someone may ask: *Is he in ?* and get the answer: *No he's out* (or, very often: *He's gone out*).
We also say: *out the back, round the back, out the front* and *round the front* meaning the front or back of the
house.

You can be: *at university, at college, at school;* but **in** *a (school) year* and *in a class* or *form; in the third year,
in class 2B, in a classroom* and *in a lesson;* or (used generally) *in class* or *in lessons;
at the airport, at the station, at the bank, at the shops* - and at particular shops: *at the supermarket, at the bakers';
at the office* and *at work* - except that *in work* means employed as distinct from unemployed (*out of work*).
Also when asked where we work we usually say *in an office,* or *in a factory* etc. - rather than *at.*

You can be: *in hospital* if you are ill, *at the hospital* if you are working there or visiting;
at the beach and *at the seaside;* but notice the distinction between *in the water* and *on the beach;
on shore* or *on land* but *in the air* (except that things you see up there are *in the sky*);
at the Wilsons' or *at a neighbours'* and *at Fred's house* (but we often say *round* or *round at* someone's house);
in the garden (or *down the garden* or *out in the garden*), *in the park, in the woods, in the country,
in the town* or simply *in town, in the neighbourhood, in the suburbs.*
You may be caught: *in the rain, in the wind, in the wet, in the snow, in a storm* or *in a heat wave.*
You stay *in a hotel* or *at a hotel,* but your room may be *on the third floor* - or simply *upstairs* or *downstairs.*
In is used for particular rooms: *in the bedroom, in the attic* etc.

In is used to locate things or places *in the sea: in the Channel, in the Atlantic, in the North Sea.*
But when you are *on a ship* (or *on board a ship*), you speak of being *at sea,* and you travel *by sea, by land,*
or *by air.* You may be *on a plane* or *on a bus,* but *in a car.* People can travel *in a lorry,* but goods go *on a lorry.*
Ships can be *in harbour* or *in port* or *in dock;* when not *in flight,* planes are *on the runway.*
Off is used for objects at sea in relation to other objects. It means something like: 'a certain distance away from'.
So: *The Orkney Islands are off the north coast of Scotland. Enemy destroyer off the port bow!*

On is used when something is located **on** *a surface: on the side, on the front, on the wall, on the floor.*
In is used when something is located **inside** *a hollow or solid object: in the cupboard, in the box.*
Look at the differences between **in** and **on** in these examples: *The picture is on the wall.
We have had insulation put in the walls. The ball hit me on the leg. I have a pain in my leg.*
Notice that we see a reflection *in the mirror,* and see something *in the distance.*
We normally sit *on a chair,* but may sit *in an armchair* (though never: 'in a sofa').
We can land *on the moon* (to see the *Man in the Moon*) or *on Mars.*
We see spots *on the sun* but sit *in the sun,* or *out in the sun,* or *in the sunshine.*

Motion is generally much simpler, in that there is usually only one word that can be used.
There are, however, still some problem words, and you should look at the examples carefully.
You can go: *from* somewhere *to* somewhere else;
along the road or *street* or *path* or *corridor*; but we often say *up the road*, or *down the road*;
across the road or *street*, or *over the road* which means much the same;
into and *out of* a *place* or *building*, *up* or *down* a hill, *over* or *under* a bridge.
You go *through* the door, but look *out of* the window (though people often say *through*).
You go *to bed*, lie *on* the bed, get *into* bed, and sleep *in* bed.
You can go *out of* or *into* the house, and put something *in* or *into* a box.
You can take something *out of* a cupboard or *out of* the country.
You put something *on* a surface (including an upright surface), and take it *off* a surface:
Hang that picture on the wall. Write it on the blackboard. Take it off the desk.
Onto is sometimes used for *on*, and we sometimes say *off of*, but plain *off* is better.
Notice: *Hang it on the peg. Take that kettle off the gas.*

There are many **other prepositions** used for place:
near, behind, under, above, over, beneath, below, beside, between, among, amid.
We also often used **groups of words** (phrases) as if they were single prepositions:
next to, out of, on top of, at the bottom of, in front of, near to, away from.

Rule 155 WITH is used in several kinds of phrase

You already know some adverb phrases of manner: those showing the agent and instrument. (Check back to
Rule 141 for this.) The **agent** is indicated using the word *by*; the **instrument** is indicated using the word *with*.
Here are some reminders of *with* used for the *instrument*:
She was stabbed with a knife. Joe cut it with the scissors. I saw it with my own eyes.

We can use *with* to indicate what something *contains*:
He filled the sack with sand. The box was packed with presents. The cart was laden with corn.
Be careful, however. We say: *filled with,* but: *full of.*
With is also used in many other adverb phrases of *manner* - phrases which tell you *how* something is done:
He spoke with a foreign accent. She went with a smile. She loved him with all her heart. Go with all speed!
These results have only been achieved with great difficulty. He has paid for it with his life.
With is often used to mean *in company with*:
She lives with her parents. I have requested a meeting with the directors. I am not going with you.
You were seen with the victim yesterday. I shall be with you shortly. I have no-one with me.
Together with is sometimes used with this meaning: *He surrendered together with his troops.*
A similar use of *with* means *regarding* or *about*:
What are you going to do with me ? I shall not put up with this. We've made no progress with the design.
Notice we use *with* meaning *against* in phrases like: *fight with, battle with.*

With is also used in *adjective phrases*, describing nouns:
The boy with the red hair and freckles did it. Bring me that book with the gold lettering on the spine.
The *opposite of with* is **without**, and this can be used in phrases similar to those above:
He turned without a glance. She is entirely without friends. Who is that boy without a tie ?

Rule 156   BY is used in several kinds of phrase

As mentioned in the last rule, you should remember the use of *by* for the *agent* of a piece of action.
Here are some examples of **by** indicating the ***agent***:
He was stabbed by his brother. Have the forms been filled in by all applicants ? He was struck by lightning.
St.Paul's was designed by Sir Christopher Wren. The pumps are operated by electricity.

By is also used together with a verbal noun, or sometimes an abstract noun, to indicate ***method***:
We can escape by crawling through the tunnel. You are condemned by your silence.
By turning down there and taking the bypass we can arrive first.

Very similar to this use is the use of **by** for ***means of communication***:
We are going by air...by sea...by land...by train....by bus (but **on** *foot* or *on horseback*).
We shall get in touch by fax...by courier...by phone (but we can also be **on** *the phone*).
Look back at *Rule 154* for how prepositions (including **by**) are used in phrases of *place*, and *153* for phrases
of *time*.

By is used to indicate what ***measurement*** is employed:
I am paid by the hour. We sell coal by the tonne. It missed me by a hair's breadth.
Notice how we use **by** for the second of two measurements: *The room is three metres by two metres.*

By is used to indicate the ***part touched*** or taken:
Hold it by the handle. I seized him by the collar. He took her by the hand.

There are some other adverb phrases of manner where **by** is used rather than **with**:
learn and know *by heart*, know *by name* or *by reputation* or *by sight*, or *by intuition*;
do something *by accident* or *by mistake* (but **on** *purpose*);
happen *by chance, by luck, by good fortune.*
By rights means *according to justice*; *by my watch* means *according to my watch.*
We also use **by** in ***oaths***: *I swear by Almighty God.....*

Rule 157   TO and FOR have several similar uses

You already know that **to** is used before the basic form of the verb as the ***infinitive***: *to go, to speak, to be.*
The **infinitive** with **to** follows many **adjectives**: *ready to go, happy to do it, good to see, nice to know, hard to*
understand, last to arrive, lucky to survive, quick to take offence, great to be alive.

To is also used for ***indirect objects*** (See *Rule 94*): *I sent it to John. Give that to me.*
For is used in a rather similar way: *I did it for you. This is for young Judy.*

There are numerous other uses of **for**, many, like *to*, following adjectives.
The following are only a few examples:
Phrases about ***destination***: *the train for Glasgow*; ***preparation***: *get ready for school; ready for anything*;
purpose (often followed by a verbal noun): *That's used for making coffee; He works for his living*;
reason: *famous for her beauty; executed for murder*; ***ability***: *an ear for music; clever for her age*;
suitability: *good for nothing; handy for the shops*; ***delegation***: *Please stand in for me tonight.*

Rule 158   Phrasal verbs often have special meanings

Phrasal verbs are verbs which are *linked* together with another word, usually a *preposition* or *adverb*.
Without the link, the verb has one meaning; with the link it often has another meaning.

English has hundreds of phrasal verbs, and it is completely impossible to do more than give a few examples to show how they work. It is important to learn their meanings as you come across them.

As an example, we shall look at the verb **to give**. **To give** means *to hand over* or *make a present*.
It is followed by an object, and sometimes also an indirect object (*To give something to someone*).
BUT:
to give way means *to retreat*: *I gave way to their demands.*
to give in means *to surrender*: *We can fight no longer; we must give in.*
to give up similarly means *to surrender* or *hand over*: *We shall have to give up the castle to Sir Boris.*
to give up also means *to abandon*: *We shall have to give up our demands for more pay.*
to give (something) *in* means *to hand over to authority*: *Give in your books at the end of the lesson.*
to give back means *to restore* (an object): *Give me back my sweets, Neil.*
to give off means *to emit* or *send out*: *The chimney gave off clouds of thick, black smoke.*
to give out means *to come to an end*: *On the eleventh day our supplies finally gave out.*
to give out also means *to distribute*, or *announce*: *The results were given out on the loudspeaker.*
to give (someone) *out* means (in cricket) *to end their innings*: *He gave Boulton out leg before wicket.*

Even then not all the phrasal verbs from *give* have been included. Some other verbs (such as *do* and *make*) have an even larger collection of phrasal verbs of this sort. Very many verbs have at least one or two.
Try to notice them while using this book, and if you do not know their meanings, check in your dictionary.

Rule 159   Avoid ending a sentence with a preposition

There used to be a rule in English that a sentence should *never* be ended with a preposition.
(As Winston Churchill put it: 'A preposition is the wrong thing to end a sentence up with....')
It is still a good idea to stick to this rule if you can, but there are exceptions.

In sentences where a verb is introduced by *what*, or *which*, or *who*, and especially in *questions* with these words, it is often necessary to end with a preposition: *What are you crying for ? Who were you talking to ?*
And: *You don't know what you are talking about* is far better than:
You do not know that about which you are talking.

Prepositions used as part of phrasal verbs, and particularly of intransitive phrasal verbs, may be put at the end (though whether such words are really prepositions rather than adverbs is a matter of opinion):
I saw them all go by. It was very late when we got in.

There are other cases where it may simply be convenient to put a preposition at the end:
He's someone worth talking to. That's the best glue for making models with (but better to leave out *with*).
He was the best speaker of the age he lived in (but the the noun phrase: *of his age* would be better).

Rule 160   The verb TO GET has several uses

Get strictly speaking means to *gain* or *acquire*. However, it is used in many other senses, and you need to know what these are. Children used to be taught only to use *get* in its basic meaning, and to find alternative words for many of the common uses. This was not a good rule, but some people still think it is important, so some alternatives are given in the examples that follow.

Get is used meaning **become**: *I got very wet today. Get well soon!*
They got married yesterday. (Alternative: *They were married yesterday.*)
Notice **get to know** meaning: *become acquainted with*: *I got to know him quite well over the years.*

Get is used meaning **make something happen**: *Get your books out, children. Did you get number four right ?*
Get out of the way! (Alternative: *Move out of the way.*)
Get out the front! (Alternative: *Come/go out to the front.*)
A similar use is in phrases like: *I can't get form four to do any work.*

Get is used with a present participle to mean **start**: *I've got it working at last.*
Notice **to get going**, which also means *start*: *Have you got it going yet. It's time we got going.*
The second example, where the verb is used intransitively is not very good English.

Get is used meaning **obtain**, **receive** or **acquire**: *I got your letter* (Alternative: *I received...*)
Have you got permission to be out of your classroom ? (A poor alternative might be: *obtained...*)
Get me an ice-cream, please. (Alternative: *buy.*) *He got a smack.* (Alternative: *was given.*)
She got told off. (Alternative: *was told off.*)

Get is used meaning **have**. This is a use that people seem to object to frequently:
I've got a lovely bunch of coconuts. (Alternative: *I have a lovely bunch of coconuts.*)
He's got more than me! (Alternative: *He has more than me.*)
I've got a cold means *I have a cold*; *I'm getting a cold* means *I am starting to catch a cold*.

I've got to is used instead of *I have to* in the same way: *I've got to go. It's got to be done.*
Got to is another usage that is unpopular with English teachers. It is still not very good English, at least in written work: *I have to go* is better than *I've got to go*.

Get is used meaning to **reach a point**, or **arrive**:
The train didn't get in till ten o'clock. (*Arrive.*) *When did you get home ?* (*Arrive.*)
I must get to bed earlier tonight. (*Go to bed.*)

There are many **phrasal verbs** of this sort formed with **get**. The following are only a very few:
Get in (arrive), get out (go out), get up (rise from a chair, bed etc.), get over (recover from),
get off (descend from a bus, train etc.), get back (return, retrieve, or move away from).

Get probably has more uses in phrasal verbs than any other verb in the language. In some of these uses with an adverb or preposition we can substitute *go* or *come* for *get*, or use an alternative expression, so long as it does not reduce the clarity of what is being said or written. Nevertheless, in written English, be careful how you use *get* in phrasal verbs, avoid repeating it, and look for alternatives. Phrasal verbs in general are less used in formal writing.

Rule 161   A clause is a group of words containing a verb

The description of a **clause** in the heading of this rule should sound rather like the description of a sentence. Sentences in nearly every case contain a verb.

However, the difference between a clause and a sentence is that a sentence always makes sense by itself; a clause on the other hand need not make sense by itself. It usually needs something else added to it. Many sentences are made up of several clauses.

A sentence may also contain several phrases. A **phrase** is different from a clause, in that it does not contain a verb (though it may well contain a verbal noun or an infinitive).

Clauses like phrases have several different **types**, and though you do not need to know their names, you should know roughly what they are when you come across them.

A clause often begins with or is introduced by a particular word, and it is always possible to separate the clause out from the rest of the sentence (though the rest may not make much sense after it is gone).

A **noun clause** does the job of a noun. So you may well find a noun clause acting as the subject or object of a sentence. Noun clauses are quite often introduced by the word *that* or by the word *what*.

For example: *There is no doubt **that he is guilty**.   He always does **what he is told**.*

An **adjective clause** does the job of an adjective. So you will find it used to describe a noun. Adjective clauses are nearly always introduced by a word like **who, which, that**.

For example: *Stand up the boy **who threw that apple**!   The one **that I wanted** has gone.*

An **adverb clause** does the job of an adverb. It is used to tell you more about the action of the verb: **how, when, where, why** etc. the action was carried out.
There are different kinds of adverb clauses, just as there are different kinds of adverb, and several of the following rules deal with them.

For example: *We have to go to bed **as soon as they arrive**.   I did not meet him **because the train was late**.*

Bear in mind the difference between a clause and a phrase.
If we take the first example given above for each of the three types of clause, in each case we could have used an equivalent phrase instead of the clause:
There is no doubt that he is guilty would be: *There is no doubt of his guilt. That he is guilty* contains a verb (*is*); *of his guilt*, however, has no verb.
Stand up the boy who threw that apple would be: *Stand up the boy responsible for throwing that apple.*
The phrase *who threw that apple* has a verb in it (*threw*); but *responsible for throwing* has no verb. *Throwing* is not a verb here, it is a verbal noun used after the preposition *for*.
We have to be in bed as soon as they arrive becomes: *We have to be in bed by the time of their arrival.*
As soon as they arrive has a verb (*arrive*); *by the time of their arrival* has two phrases linked together and introduced by the prepositions *by* and *of*.
Sometimes in your own writing it is best to use a clause, sometimes a phrase.
Pick the one that is simplest and clearest.

Rule 162   A noun clause does the job of a noun

Noun clauses are often introduced by **that**, with a statement of fact following. You could often begin them with
the words: *the fact that*. Noun clauses can be used in the same way as nouns. They are more often used as the
object of a sentence than as the subject. Here are some examples of noun clauses:
That she should have suffered so much is a terrible tragedy. It's not fair that only Douglas should be punished.
Please ensure that everything is ready. It is not my fault that we can't afford it. It so happens that I saw it all.

Even in cases where you might expect a noun clause as subject, it is more usual to turn the sentence round. This
can be done by starting the sentence with *it* - to make the noun clause a complement after the verb *to be*, or the
object:
That I may be killed on this expedition does not worry me - Noun clause (*that I may be killed*) subject.
It does not worry me that I may be killed on this expedition - *It* as subject; the noun clause now object.
It is quite common to **leave out** the word **that** when a noun clause follows a verb:
I'd heard you were much better (rather than: *that you were much better*).

We also sometimes prefer to use noun phrases with the infinitive or a verbal noun rather than a noun clause.
That I may be thought a coward does worry me - noun clause subject.
Being thought a coward does worry me - noun phrase used as the subject.

Noun clauses may also be introduced by the word **what**. Once again they may be subject or object:
What you decide to do is no concern of mine. What I may want has never troubled you. (Subject of the sentence.)
You know what I think about your suggestion. I know what I like and I like what I know. (Object.)

Noun clauses introduced by **what** are much more common as the **subject** than those introduced by *that*.
If a noun clause of this sort is the subject of the verb, it must be followed by a singular verb:
What I like is sweets, and plenty of them (*is* not *are*). Compare this with: *Sweets are what I like.*

Noun clauses may also follow **prepositions**:
I support him in what he has done. In that you have acted improperly, I cannot support you.

Rule 163   The relative pronoun has several forms

You need to learn about the relative pronoun now because the relative pronoun is what begins adjective clauses.
In fact **adjective clauses** are more usually called **relative clauses**. The relative pronoun nearly always plays an
essential part in its own clause - usually as the subject or object of the verb in the clause

WHO is the **subject** form, singular and plural - for use with **people**: *These are the people who wanted to see you.*
WHOM is the **object** form, singular and plural - for use with people: *This is the boy whom you wished to see.*
WHOM is the form used **after prepositions** (with people): *He is the boy about whom we were speaking.*
But in nearly all *spoken English*, and often in written English as well:
WHO may be used **to replace WHOM**: *Is he the one who you wanted to see ?*

WHOSE is the **possessive** form of **WHO**: *He is the one whose pen was stolen.*
Whose is sometimes used for *things* as well as for people: *It is an idea whose power will never fade.*

WHICH is the **subject** and **object** form, singular and plural - for use with **things**: *Is this the pen which he stole ?*
WHICH is also used after prepositions; the only **possessive** form is **OF WHICH**: *Is it the one of which I spoke ?*

THAT may used **instead of** *WHO/WHOM* and *WHICH*: *He's not the one that we saw.*
That does not have any different forms and you cannot put a preposition in front of it in this usage.

Rule 164 Some relative clauses are introduced by the pronoun THAT

There are two sorts of relative clause. The first sort is a *defining* or *limiting relative clause*.
A **defining clause** gives essential information. If the defining relative clause were left out, the sentence would make very little sense or seem entirely pointless. Rather similar is a limiting relative clause.
A **limiting clause** makes it much more clear which particular item is being described. It is not really adding information, more cutting down the possibilities
Defining or limiting relative clauses are generally introduced by **that**:
This is the book that I was looking for. He's the one that did it. Where is the statue that you mentioned ?
Those boys that damaged the telephone box should be made to pay for it. The name that he gave was a false one.
Did the letter that came this morning contain the cheque that you were expecting.

A defining or limiting relative clause follows directly from the rest of the sentence.
It should *not* be *separated* from it *by commas*.

There are some *cases when* **that** *is not used* in defining or limiting relative clauses.
We do **not** use *that* **after a preposition**. We have to use **which** or **whom**:
The man for whom I was looking has gone. Is this the book for which I asked?
Notice that we could write: *The man that I was looking for has gone*, and, if we don't mind ending a sentence with a preposition: *Is this the book that I asked for ?*

There is **no possessive of *that***, so we must use *of which* or **whose**:
He is the one whose name was called. It is the house of which we saw the photograph.
(In the second example: *It is the house that we saw the photograph of* is probably better.)

Even in defining and limiting relative clauses, we regularly use **who *instead of* that** when the clause is describing a person or **people**: *The man who attacked me was wearing a mask. People who wish to leave may do so now.*
In these cases *that* would not be wrong, but *who* is rather more common.

We nearly always **use *who*** in the following cases:
After a noun (used for a person) which is linked with *any*, *only* or *all*:
You are the only one who could have managed it. All those who saw it please come forward.
After a noun (used for a person) that is the complement of *it is/it was*:
It was one of those boys who were running down the street. It's the wife who makes the decisions.

When **that** is the **object** in this sort of relative clause, it is very often **missed out** altogether:
These are the people [that] I told you about. The pen [that] you gave me is broken already.
Where is this new house [that] you were telling me about ? That's the man [that] we met in Paris ?

Notice that we generally *do not use* **whom** in defining and limiting relative clauses. You might have expected *whom* in the last of the four examples just given, since it is about a person. *Whom* is correct, but less common..
Instead we use *that*, or we leave *that* out and use nothing, or sometimes we even use *who*.
Also notice that we often prefer to use **that** rather than *when* after a stated **time**:
It was during the time that I was commissioner. We first met the evening that we saw 'Iolanthe'.

Finally, do not become confused by other uses of *that*.
That can be an **adjective**. *It's that man again.*
That can be a **pronoun**: *That's the way to do it.*
That can introduce **noun clauses** as well as adjective clauses: *It is undeniable that she is sufficiently intelligent.*

Rule 165   Some relative clauses are introduce by WHO or WHICH

You already know about one sort of relative clause: the **defining or limiting clause**, which is introduced by: **that.**
As explained in *Rule 164*, **who** is sometimes used *in place* of **that**, as in:
He is the one who spoke to me. The woman who was waiting was Miss Green. Anyone who wants to can come in.
Which is also sometimes used in this sort of relative clause, but is much less common.

However, sentences like the following examples are not wrong:
The Atlantic is the ocean which separates Europe and America. Is this the book which you were reading ?
Also, since **that** is *not used with a preposition*, and has *no possessive form*, you have to use the various forms
of *who* and *which* in its place:
by which, with which, at which, of which, by whom, with whom, of whom and *whose.*

The second sort of relative clause is the **descriptive clause**. The sentence would survive without it being there.
You can take it away and the sentence still means something (though not so much). Also, once the relative clause
has been removed, it should be possible to make it into a sentence of its own without any trouble.
Look at this example:
The captain, who was determined to go down with his ship, ordered the crew to man the lifeboats. Now if we take
out the relative clause we still have a perfectly good sentence: *The captain ordered the crew to man the lifeboats.*
We can also use the relative clause, with hardly any change, to make a second sentence to follow it:
He was determined to go down with his ship. The relative pronoun simply becomes a personal pronoun.

A descriptive relative clause is very often **separated** from the rest of the sentence by a **comma before** the relative
pronoun, and another **comma at the end** of the clause. Use these two commas particularly if it is a long relative
clause. You can leave them out if it is short. Do not put one of them in and leave the other out.

A **descriptive relative clause** should **use *who* or *which*** rather than *that*.

As you should already know, **who** is used as the **subject** of the relative clause and mainly for **people**:
Mr Jackson, who has been with the firm for thirty years, will be retiring next month.
I must introduce you to young Perkins, who has been away on a course recently.

Whom is used instead of *who* as the **object** of the relative clause:
Young Perkins, whom we both met on Thursday, has applied for another course.
The manager, whom you described in the canteen as a complete idiot, would like a moment of your time.

Whom is also used **after a preposition**:
Mr Sawyer, to whom we offer our hearty congratulations, has been elected leader of the council.
The three mountaineers, with whom I spoke only yesterday, are now feared dead.

Whose is used to indicate **possession** or ownership:
Young Perkins, whose absences are becoming irritating, is off again today.
The boy whose ball broke my window this morning had better come and see me now.

Remember that *whose* means *of whom*; *who's* means *who is* or *who has*.

Which is used for **things** rather than people, and **does not change** its form. It can be the subject or object of the relative clause, or used after a pronoun. It has no possessive form; we have to say: *of which*.

Here are examples of all these uses:
The council, which has just elected Sawyer as its new leader, will be meeting tomorrow.
The leave of absence, which I only granted to you with reluctance, will not be extended, Perkins.
The house, for which we paid a hundred thousand, is now only worth half that.
This ball, the owner of which has not come forward, will remain in my office.

Notice in the last example that we switch the **order** to: **subject** of relative clause, plus **relative pronoun** plus **preposition**. This is normally done, in phrases like: *a question, the answer to which....; a proposal, the reason for which...; an atrocity, the like of which...*etc.
It is uncommon to leave the order as: *This ball of which the owner.....*

Which and *who* have another use in asking *questions*, in addition to those as relative pronouns.
Which may introduce questions as an adjective: *Which girls want to come ? Which subject do you like best ?*
Which and *who* may be used as interrogative pronouns: *Which is it to be ? Who wants an ice-cream?*

Whoever and *whichever* can be used as pronouns or adjectives to mean:
the one which/the one who, or *no matter which/no matter who*:
Whichever way I turn I am still lost (adjective). *Whoever is responsible had better own up* (pronoun).

What is a shortened form of **that which** in sentences like: *I know what you've been doing*; and: *What I've been doing is no concern of yours*. So we could classify clauses starting with *what* as relative clauses, rather than noun clauses. Remember that if they are the subject of the main sentence they need a singular verb.

Whatever means: *no matter what, everything which, anything which*; and, as an adjective, *of any kind*.
For example: *Whatever you do, don't tell her. I promise to do whatever I can. Take whatever steps are necessary.*

Rule 166 Nouns and noun phrases may be used in apposition

Nouns and noun phrases used in apposition are a little like relative clauses without a relative pronoun.
When a noun or noun phrase is put in **apposition** it is simply placed next to another noun (or another noun phrase), to give an *additional piece of information* about that noun. Very often it is another name or title for the noun being described. Nouns and noun phrases in apposition are generally separated from the rest of the sentence by commas before and after.

In this sentence: *The Reverend Dawes preached today*, we could add a piece of information by putting a noun phrase in apposition: *The Reverend Dawes, the Vicar of St. James', preached today.*
Similarly: *I noticed that Sinclair had come in* can be expanded by the use of words in apposition to:
I noticed that Sinclair, a shady and disreputable character, had come in.

In both these examples we could have used *who is* to introduce the words put in apposition, and so changed them into a relative clause. However, the use of apposition is shorter and often better, when we are simply adding a short piece of additional information.

Rule 167   Adverbial clauses of place describe where actions occur

This type of adverbial clause is not in fact particularly common, because information about WHERE can usually be given more easily in the form of a phrase.
They are generally introduced by (i.e. they start with) **where** or **wherever**:
Stand over there where I can see you.   That cat always hides where you'd least expect her to.
They were lying in wait for us where the woods are thickest. We can go wherever you want.

Notice the old fashioned words: *whence*, meaning *where from*, and *whither* meaning *where to*.
We now virtually always say ***where from*** and ***where to***, even when this means ending a sentence with a preposition:
Where have you come from and where are you going (to)? not:
Whence have you come and whither are you going.

Where is also used to ask questions, as you know (*Rule 106.*).

Rule 168   Temporal clauses describe when actions occur

A temporal clause is the correct name for an adverb clause of time, which tells you WHEN the action of the verb happens. Unlike clauses of place, adverb clauses of time are very common indeed. They are also very simple, and should present no problems.
As you would expect these clauses are very often introduced by the word **when**, but there are many similar words:
after, whenever, while, until, till, before, since.
For example:
I had a shock when I saw him there. We finally started after he had arrived. Have a drink before you go.
All the food was finished before we arrived. Whenever I pass that door I always tremble.
While you have been playing, I have been hard at work. He has lived there since the house was built.
Wait here till I tell you to leave. I waited until I was told to leave.

The meanings of *when*, *before* and *after* are obvious.

Whenever means something like: ***every time that***.

Till and **until** have exactly the same meaning as each other.
They set an ***end limit*** on the time of something that is already happening or just about to happen.

While is used to mean ***during*** a particular action (sometimes called ***time throughout***).

Be careful using **since**. It can mean ***all the time from a start point*** (rather like the reverse of *until*).
However, **since** can also be used to mean ***because.*** (See *Rule 173* below.)

Sometimes temporal clauses are introduced by a group of words, particularly *as soon as*, and *as long as*.
As soon as means ***when***, but refers to something ***due to happen***: *We can go as soon as you are ready.*
As long as is used for ***time throughout*** again: *I will stay as long as you want me to.*

However, be careful with this expression. **As long as** and **so long as** are also used to mean ***provided that*** or ***on the condition that***. See *Rule 174* below about this use.

When and **whenever** can also be used for ***asking questions***.

Rule 169   The result of an action is described in a consecutive clause

You may find it easier to think of these as **result clauses**, though the name 'consecutive' merely means that they state the 'consequence'. The simplest form of consecutive clause is introduced by the word **so**:
The shop was shut, so I couldn't get any fish. He has been well looked after, so he should recover soon.
It was already late, so I went to bed. We went abroad last year, so this year we're staying at home.

So has many other uses, as well as telling the result, and you will find that it is also used in purpose clauses, as explained in *Rule 172*. However, it has another use in describing the result or consequence,
where **so *plus adverb or adjective*** is followed by **that** and a consecutive clause:
I was so tired that I fell asleep at once. We ran so fast that we caught the bus after all.
They had repeated the task so often that they could do it in their sleep.
So far from is used to express an opposite: *He was so far from competent that I dismissed him yesterday.*
We use: **Far from it !** to mean: *Oh no, the opposite is true.*

There is a variation of this usage, where *so* is replaced by **such**. We use **such** with an adjective plus a noun:
He is such a naughty boy that I have asked his father to punish him. They were such a bargain that I bought two.
They are such clever girls that they have been moved into a higher class.
Notice the order: such (plus indefinite article) plus adjective plus noun.
Such always goes first in this sort of phrase: *That is such a pretty dress !*

We can also employ a phrase using **too**, often plus an **infinitive**, to express result or consequence:
That is too good to be true. You were too busy to do your homework, were you ?
That is too ridiculous for words (meaning: *so ridiculous that it cannot be adequately described*).
Remember that the first **too** has two *o*'s, and the second **to** has one *o*.

Rule 170   The manner of an action may be described in a comparative clause

Adverbs of manner, which tell you HOW an action is carried out, are probably the most common. The vast majority of the adverbs that end in **ly** are adverbs of manner. Adverb phrases of manner are also very common. Perhaps for this reason, the only adverb clauses of manner tell us how the action occurred by means of a **comparison**, and are therefore called **comparative clauses**.

The basic comparative clause is introduced by **as**:
He is not fit to be Prime Minister, as his predecessor was. We worked as we had never worked before.
In this sort of sentence **as** means something like *in the way that*.

We do not use this very simple form of comparative clause much, and when we do use it, we often get it wrong.
As must be used to introduce a **comparative clause** (a comparison that has a **verb**).
Like is generally used to introduce a **comparative phrase** (**no verb**).
So: *I waited, as one who knows his fate is sealed, until the count entered like a fiend from Hell.*
To have written: *like one who knows his fate is sealed* in this example would strictly speaking, have been wrong, though it is now very common at least in spoken English.
It would also have been wrong to have written *as a fiend from Hell* for the comparative phrase.

We can use **as** in some **comparative phrases**. It is used to mean *playing the part of* or *taking the place of*:
Miss Martin appeared as Queen Titania. He stood in for me as chairman of the meeting.

Be careful with the other use of **as** to mean *because*.
The second example on the previous page might possibly be read in this way.
(*We worked because we had never worked before* not: *We worked in a way that we had never worked before.*)
Where there is a possible misunderstanding, try to rewrite your sentence in a different form.
It is generally possible to substitute an adverbial phrase of comparison, with *like*, for the clause.

Comparative clauses may be introduced by **as if** and **as though**:
We ran as if a monster was chasing us. You look as though you could do with a drink.
He was speaking as if he was in a daze. He looked as though a lorry had hit him.
As if and **as though** may also be followed by an **infinitive** to make a phrase rather than a clause:
He opened his mouth as if to say something.

Many clauses and phrases using **as if** strongly suggest what we could call an **unreal comparison**.
If you look at the first four examples above, you can safely assume that there was no monster chasing in the first,
and no traffic accident in the last. In the phrase *as if to say something*, we get a clear idea that as a matter
of fact nothing was said.
Just as if makes the unreal comparison even clearer: *He sat there staring at me just as if he was still alive.*

As if is also used for **future possibilities**: *It looks as if we're going to win.*
In spoken English the incorrect form: *It looks like we're going to win* is also commonly used.

We use **it is not as if** (or sometimes only **as if**), when we want to rule out a possible excuse:
It isn't as if he didn't know he had homework. It's not as if they're too poor to buy one.
As if you didn't know better!

If you are using a **comparative phrase** in which a pronoun follows the word *than*, the pronoun is usually in its
object form: *better than me, more than him, slower than us, faster than them, prettier than her.*

If you are using a **comparative clause**, pronouns which are the *subject* of the clause will have their subject form:
better than I am, more than he did, slower than we were, faster than they did, prettier than she was.

Sometimes you see expressions like: *He is better than I* (rather than: *He is better than me.*). These are not wrong.
What is happening is that the writer is starting a clause, but missing out the verb because it is obvious.

Occasionally using *than* followed by a simple pronoun can be very confusing.
You like her better than me means: *You like her better than you like me*
However, it might also mean: *You like her better than I like her.*
If in doubt, use the clause you mean in full, rather than the phrase with just the pronoun.

We can **combine *as* and *than*** comparisons when we are comparing three or more things:
She is taller than Robert, but not as tall as Jenny. He's the same age as me, but younger than you.
We can also use opposite comparatives in three-way comparisons:
He's older than me, but younger than my brother.
Remember the use of the comparative and superlative in comparing three or more:
Jack is faster than Joe, and Bill is the fastest. I walked more slowly than you, but Wendy was the slowest.

Finally we can make a simile by using two **opposing comparatives**:
The bigger they are, the harder they fall. The longer I waited, the thirstier I became.

Rule 171   Comparisons may be made by means of a simile

A **simile** (pronounced sim-ill-ee) is an expression which says that **one thing is like another**.
Similes can be both clauses and phrases, and to simplify things we shall look at both in this rule.
One sort of **simile** uses **like**:
He eats like ten men. She's been behaving like a spoilt child. Your eyes are like limpid pools in the moonlight.
The avalanche enveloped them like a cold white winding sheet. He looked like a ghost.
In all these examples *like* is rather similar to a preposition introducing a descriptive phrase. In written English do
not use *like* to begin a clause. The correct use of *like* and *as* is explained in *Rule 170*. Check back to make sure you
know the two usages, as in: *It looks like rain* and *It looks as if it is going to rain.*

Sometimes we use **compared with** to make a direct comparison:
Compared with young Smedley's work, yours is very poor, Marge. You're brilliant compared with me.
Compared with is very often used to make an *unfavourable comparison*.
The verb *to compare to* simply means to make a comparison: *He compared Stalin to Hitler.*

Another sort of **simile** uses **as** followed by **as**:
It's as pretty as a picture. Your hands are as cold as ice. This box is as heavy as lead.
Expressions like the examples here, where the comparison is used to add to the descriptive power of an adjective,
are traditional, and most of them have been in use for many years.
You can, however, make up new ones if you want to: *Your computer's as old as an abacus.*
Similar comparisons using adverbs are rarer, but still quite possible: *He was walking as slowly as a snail.*
Sometimes in well known similes, we **leave out** the first **as**: *You're sharp as a tack, aren't you ?*

Ordinary adverb **clauses** of comparison can also be formed using **as.....as**:
Take as much as you want. They can stay as long as they like. We tried as hard as we could.
Get as far away from here as you possibly can. I have given as detailed a summary as I am able.
In these clauses, the verbs are very often of the same sort as those used in the examples above:
can and *could, want, like, wish, choose, need, dare* (all of which are regularly followed by an infinitive).
Notice what happened in the last of the above examples to the words: *a detailed summary;* when *as* was put in
front of the phrase, it became *as detailed a summary.*

We can directly compare two people or things using **as.....as**:
You're as good as me. She's nearly as tall as her sister. The Eiffel Tower is not as tall as the CN Tower.

The above are all phrases, but it also works using clauses in the comparison:
I can throw it just as far as you can. Fred does not swim quite as well as his brother does.
Notice that in the comparison the verb is stated in a form which just uses the auxiliary.
The same as can be used in the same way: *You're as old as me* or *You're the same age as me.*

If we want to compare **unequals**, we use the **comparative plus *than***.
Read through *Rules 44* to *48* on the comparative forms of adjectives, and *Rule 136* on the comparative of adverbs,
to remind you how they work. Then look at these examples of comparisons with *than*:
He is taller than his brother. His answers were better than Susan's. You walk much faster than me.
Mary sings more sweetly than Jane. That is far better than anyone else's efforts.
All the above examples use phrases (or single words) for the comparison. The following use clauses:
I worked much harder than he did. Sarah has made a better choice than I expected she would.
Taylor works harder at his maths than he does in English. You have more ability than I shall ever have.
Once again, we use an auxiliary, rather than repeating the verb. *I work much harder than he works*
is not wrong; *I work much harder than he does* is the more common usage.

94

Rule 172   The aim or purpose of an action is described in a final clause

This sort of clause states the reason why an action is done - so it gives the **final** aim or purpose.
If you prefer, you can call them *purpose* clauses.

The way to state the **purpose** in a clause is by using **in order that**:
We eat in order that we may live. We work hard in order that we may succeed.
In order that is very occasionally shortened to *that*: *We eat that we may live.*

In order that is sometimes **replaced by** *so that*: *We work hard so that we may succeed.*

However, the easiest way to express the **purpose** of an action is to use a simple **infinitive**, rather than a
final clause.
The infinitive follows the main part of the sentence, and is all that you need:
We eat to live.   We work hard to succeed.   We went there to see Mr Hodgkinson.   She did it to spite Sheila.
The defendant claimed that he had only stolen to help out his poor sick mother.
The bomb was planted to create the maximum possible destruction.

The use of the infinitive to express purpose is very similar to its use after some verbs like: *want to, try to, hope to.*
Check back to *Rule 121* for these verbs.

In your own writing, you should generally use the simple method with the infinitive to express aim or purpose.

Rule 173   The cause of the action is stated in a causal clause.

Causal clauses are among the simplest.
We generally state the **cause** by using the word **because**:
Because you have seen that note, you will have to die. He fled the country because he was in debt.
I am here because you sent for me. He only married her because she was rich.

We also use **because of** followed by a **phrase** to give causes:
He only married her because of her money.

As well as *because*, **since** is sometimes used to state the **cause**:
Since you are responsible, you will have to pay the penalty.

Be careful with **since**; it is also used in temporal clauses to set a **start time**:
Since I refuse to give him any money, he hates me. (Causal clause, explaining the reason for the action.)
He has hated me since I refused to give him some money. (Temporal clause, explaining when the action began.)

As is used in causal clauses, which can also be confusing as it has so many other uses:
As Mary got top marks in the test, she can go home early.

For is sometimes used to introduce causal clauses: *I cannot go, for I am afraid of the master.*
However, **for** is more commonly used to introduce **phrases** that give an explanation for the action:
I cannot go for fear of my master. He did it for the best of motives.

Rule 174   Conditional clauses are introduced by IF

A **conditional** or 'if' clause, sets **conditions** or **limitations** on the action.
There are various sorts of conditions, but the main distinction between them is as follows:
some are **possible**, some are **impossible**, and some are **hypothetical**.

Possible conditions may be in past, present or future time:
If you were at the shops yesterday, you may have seen me. If he goes out, come and tell us at once.
If you are coming, could you let me know. If you are in there, you had better open the door right now.
If I see him tomorrow, I'll ask him to get in touch with you. If you have made a mistake, you must correct it.
The verbs in the **if** clauses are in the past or present tense depending on the time.
Notice, however, that we even tend to use the **present tense** for possible conditions set in the **future**.

Impossible conditions are set in **past** time and refer to something that **did not happen**:
If you had been to the shops yesterday, you would have seen me. If I hadn't done it I'd be a free man now.
Notice that we tend to use the **pluperfect tense** (with *had*) for these conditions.
Also the **main verb** nearly always follows the auxiliary modal verb *would*. (See *Rule 128*.)

Hypothetical conditions often have the simple form of the past tense.
Hypothetical (said: hi -po -thet -ick -al) means something like *imaginary* or *invented*.
When we say hypothetical things we often start with the words: *What if....*
Here are some examples of hypothetical conditions:
Do you think he would give me a rise if I asked him nicely?
If you were on the moon you wouldn't be able to breathe.
In hypothetical, as in impossible, conditions, the main verb of the sentence often has **would** as its auxiliary.
The verb in the **if clause** is often in the **past tense**.
The use of **even if** is explained in *Rule 175*.

This rule gives the basic version of what tenses to use in conditions. There is some more information about the
correct use of tenses in *Rule 183*, which you may want to look at now.

We often use **unless** instead of **if not**:
If you do not stop it you will be in trouble means the same as: *Unless you stop it you will be in trouble.*

If only is used to express a wish: *If only I pass the exam next week! If only I had asked her name!*
Notice that one wish is possible (present tense, about future time) and the other impossible (pluperfect tense,
about past time).

Somewhere between a conditional clause and a concessive clause (which is described in the next rule)
is what we might call a **proviso**.
This deliberately sets a condition, and is very often introduced by one of of these phrases:
provided that, on (the) condition that or **only if**.
Here are some examples:
I will carry out your instructions, provided that you put them in writing. He says he will only do it if you agree.
On the condition that my men are not held prisoner, I will hand over the fort.

Rule 175 Concessive clauses are introduced by ALTHOUGH or THOUGH

Though and **although** both mean something like: *in spite of*. There is no difference between the two words, and you may use either *though* or *although* as you wish. Here are some examples:
Though you hate me, I still love you. Although it's the middle of winter, he was playing outside with no coat.
Although we were in India, we did not see the Himalayas. Though you may torture me, I shall never tell you.
Though I had often written to her in the past she had never replied. Although Mary won't go, Jim will.

We sometimes use other words, particularly **even if**, to introduce concessive clauses:
Even if he apologized, I wouldn't have spoken to him. I like him, even if you don't.
***However much** you cry, I still shan't let you out* is rather similar.

Though and **although** can also introduce a **phrase** rather than a clause:
He's very intelligent, though rather shy. The supplies were very welcome, although too late for many people.

Rule 176 Conjunctions may join words or parts of sentences

The use of conjunctions is not difficult. **Conjunctions** are **joining words**.
You are already familiar with them in their use to join two or more single words.
You have also been learning a great deal about how they are used to link a clause to the rest of the sentence. Most of the words which introduce clauses are in fact classified as conjunctions.

The conjunctions have been clearly shown in the following examples of different types of clause:
*We waited **until** they had gone. **After** the train went, she was still on the platform. Whistle **while** you work.*
*I expect you'll find them **where** you put them. He's as daft **as** a brush. Turn the light off **as** you go out.*
***As** you are here, I'll show you the office. He was so tired **that** he could hardly keep his eyes open.*
*He did it **in order to** help his friend. I wanted it **because** she had one. **If** I try for it, will you help me ?*
***Since** you cannot explain it, I must assume you are responsible. You've changed **since** I last saw you.*
*I will carry on, **even if** all my friends desert me. **Although** she is old, her memory has not failed.*
Notice that when the clause comes before the main part of the sentence, the the conjunction comes first.
Also notice that some words used as conjunctions may have other uses as other parts of speech.

Of course there are much simpler uses of conjunctions:
*I went out of the back door **and** strolled down the garden. I don't think he saw me, **but** he may have.*
In fact **and** and **but** are the two commonest conjunctions, since they are used for joining parts of sentences
and for joining pairs of words.
Remember that if you have a list of ***three or more*** items (whether it is three or more pieces of a sentences; or three or more nouns, or three or more adjectives or adverbs), then **and** is only used ***between the last two***. The others are generally separated only by a comma. The ***comma before the final*** and is often ***missed out***, but if you are joining three parts of a sentence, and the result is rather long and complicated, you may well want to put it in.
So: *It was a long, slow and weary journey. Make sure you bring boots, a scarf and an anorak.*
He opened the door, looked round a few times and then stepped out.

Notice that **then** is not really a conjunction. It is very common in spoken English to say things like:
Just come up here, then you'll see it. Strictly speaking we should say ***and then***, or write two separate sentences.
It is still best to do so in written English: *Come up here and then you'll see it* or: *Come up here. Then you'll see it.*

Exercise 54

Where there is a noun in bold (heavy) print in these sentences put one of the personal pronouns in its place.
Make sure you use the right form depending on whether the noun is subject or object.
(1) **Susan** saw **the man**.   **The man** was holding **the dog** by the collar. **The dog** was barking loudly.
(2) **Marcus** shouted to **the soldiers. The soldiers** were watching **the scene**, but **the soldiers** ignored **the boy**.

Exercise 55

Choose the correct word from the choices given you in these sentences:
(1) It is there/their/they're house.   (2) Which house is your/yours one, and which is there's/their/theirs ?
(3) There's/theirs a cold wind tonight.   (4) She says it's/its hers/her book.
(5) He and I are/am going out later.   (6) She and Peter are/is coming.
(7) One of them is/are responsible.   (8) Is/are anyone at home ?

Exercise 56

(1) Write two sentences, the first using *this* as an adjective, the second using *this* as a pronoun.
(2) Do the same thing for *these*, *that*, and *those*.
(3) Write two sentences, one using *here* and the other using *there* as the subject of the verb.

Exercise 57

For these sentences, write down each separate **phrase**.
Then say whether it is a noun phrase, adjective phrase or adverb phrase.
(1) Under the oak tree, with its leafy branches, we sat down for a rest after our long walk.
(2) The decision to leave, finally taken today, will be told to the management as soon as possible.
(3) Chattering unwarily, the members of the fourth form strolled into the abode of the mad science teacher.
(4) Heedless of the pain, valiant to the last, he leapt for the chandelier, his trusty broadsword still in hand.
(5) To write a play is a much more serious business than writing a book; writing a book is, by comparison, simple.

Exercise 58

(1) Write a sentence using **for** to indicate length of time.
(2) Write a sentence which states a particular time by the clock.
(3) Write a sentence in which a latest time is stated.
(4) Write a sentence indicating that something will happen on the afternoon of the following day.
(5) Write a sentence in which a start time is stated.

Exercise 59

Insert the correct preposition from *in*, *at* and *on* in front of each of the following words.
If more than one could be used, try to explain any difference in meaning between the possible alternatives.
(1) the beach   (2) home   (3) the pavement   (4) the mirror   (5) England
(6) top   (7) the rain (8) school   (9) work   (10) the fourth floor

Exercise 60

Insert the correct preposition from *by*, *with*, *to*, *for* and *of* in the following sentences.
(1) He is standing in .... the chairman.   (2) We have an agreement .... the bank.
(3) The tank is full .... water. It was filled .... the top....... water .... Mr Joblins.
(4) I will not put up .... this .... a moment longer. (5) .... chance, I knew him .... sight.

Exercise 61
Using a dictionary, or your own knowledge, give the meaning of the following phrasal verbs:
(1) play down   (2) put by   (3) hand down   (4) cover up   (5) cross out
(6) pencil in   (7) go off   (8) pass out   (9) sign off   (10) turn over
You should find more than one meaning for quite a few of these. Give all the possibilities.

Exercise 62
Write down each subordinate clause in the following sentences and say whether it is a noun clause, an adjective (relative) clause, or an adverbial clause.
(1) Although I objected, they have decided that they will appoint the candidate who is in fact least qualified.
(2) Once he had seen me, whoever he might be, he clearly decided that I was the one he was looking for.
(3) Whatever he wanted was given to him as soon as he made known his wish.
(4) Because he was waiting in the doorway, I could not, despite my best efforts, get away until much later.

Exercise 63
Go back to your answers for the last exercise.
(a) For each adverbial clause, say what particular sort of adverbial clause it is.
(b) For each relative clause, state the person or thing the clause describes.
(c) For each noun clause, state whether it is subject or object of the sentence.

Exercise 64
Insert the most suitable form of the relative pronoun in the following sentences.
(1) To who/whom/which have I the honour of speaking, sir ?
(2) The boy, who/that/which/whom was definitely wearing a school blazer, ran off when I saw him.
(3) Jones is the only one who/which/that/*no pronoun* can do the job properly.
(4) Look, there's the picture which/that/*no pronoun* I told you about.
(5) The book for which/for that I was searching has vanished completely.

Exercise 65
For each question, write a sentence of your own which uses the kind of adverbial clause stated:
(1) adverb clause of place   (2) temporal (time) clause   (3) consecutive (result) clause
(4) comparative clause with *as if*   (5) final (purpose) clause.

Exercise 66
Now try to rewrite your own sentences from the last exercise, in each case replacing the clause with a phrase. You should aim to keep as closely as possible to your original meaning.

Exercise 67
Write the usual word or words of comparison used in these similes:
(1) as green as   (2) as bright as   (3) as sharp as   (4) as deaf as   (5) as heavy as
(6) as fresh as   (7) as silent as   (8) as hungry as   (9) as happy as   (10) as clean as.
Give more than one answer if you can.

Exercise 68
Write three sentences of your own using the following kinds of conditional clause:
(a) A possible condition   (b) an impossible condition (c) a hypothetical condition.

But, unlike *and*, is used to distinguish from each other the items it links together. Words, or parts of sentences following *but* are always different from what has gone before, stating a **contrast** or very often the direct opposite: *She was poor, but she was honest. I like her, but she hates me. It is a difficult task, but worth it in the end.*

Sometimes we want to put some sort of link word in a new sentence to connect it with what has gone before. It is not wrong to **start** a new sentence **with** *and* or *but*. However, some people think it is wrong - and they may be the ones who mark your English exams ! Therefore, you should use alternative link words - and several are available.

Instead of *and* you can use an adverb like: **furthermore** or **moreover.** (In spoken English the equivalent is the phrase: **what is more.**) **Therefore** is a useful way of starting a new sentence which gives the result of what has gone before; **accordingly** is often used in the same way. **Hence** can be used to mean *therefore*; so can **thus** - but save them for very formal writing. So: *The chairman is not present. Therefore the meeting cannot start.*

We more often like to **contrast** a new sentence with the one that has gone before, rather than merely link it. If we are to avoid starting with *but*, the best word to use is **however.** *However* sometimes goes as the first word, but sometimes comes after the subject, or even after the first phrase in a longer sentence. **Nevertheless** and **notwithstanding** can also be used as substitutes for *but*. You can also tack **though** onto the end of a short sentence with the same result.
So: *Nevertheless, there is a majority in support of the proposal. It is, however, only a small majority.*
Mr Blenkinsop is determined to force this issue, though. However, it is too important a matter to be hurried.
Most of these link words are often classified as **adverbs** - but they behave very like **conjunctions.**

Rule 177   Some conjunctions are used in pairs

You already recognise some words that operate in pairs:
As.....as: *He is as thin as a rake.*
So.....that: *It was so fast that I hardly saw it.*
There are several pairs of conjunctions which work in a rather similar way.

Either.....or..... is used as a lengthened form of the simple *or*.
Either.....or..... should be used only when there are just *two* possible alternatives (though in fact it is sometimes used for three, with a second *or*). For example: *Either Tom or Bill should come with us.*
Either the boys will have to share or we shall have to ask for a larger room.
Neither.....nor..... is used in the same way in the *negative*:
Neither the Prime Minister nor the Chancellor was in the House.
We shall neither surrender to their demands, nor abandon our own interests.

Both.....and..... is used as a stronger form of *and*:
Both Bill and Tom should come with us. Both using a pen and using a typewriter are equally out of date.
Not only......but also..... is a stronger form of *both....and....*, tending to stress the second item:
Not only her parents came to the party, but also her entire family.

There is often confusion about whether the **verb** should be **singular or plural** when there is a subject formed by two persons or things linked by a paired conjunction in this way. A rule to cover this problem follows.

Rule 178 Subjects linked by conjunctions may take singular or plural verbs

There are often difficulties in knowing whether a plural or a singular verb is required when the subject comes in two parts, linked by a conjunction.

In general, the link word for a two-part subject will be **and**. In this case the subject is plural and a plural verb is required. There is no possible difficulty. So: *A pen **and** a note book **are** essential for a train-spotter.*

Both.....and..... behaves exactly **the same as** a simple **and**.
If either section in *both.....and.....* is plural, the verb must be plural.
If both the sections in *both.....and.....* are singular, the verb is still plural. The reason is in fact obvious. All that we are doing is linking two singular items with a rather stronger form of *and*: and singular plus singular equals plural! For example: *Both Michael and his mother were waiting for us at the bus stop.*

However, **not only.....but also.....** does not behave so reasonably.
The verb is **singular or plural** depending on whether the **part of the subject nearest** to it is singular or plural.
So: *Not only all the children but also their teacher **is** coming on the trip.*
This does not sound quite right, however, and there is a simple way to get round it.
Arrange sentences of this sort, where one half of the subject is singular and the other half plural, in such a way that the plural part is nearest the verb: *Not only their teacher, but also all the children are coming on the trip.*

A slightly different arrangement applies to subjects joined by **or**, to subjects joined by **either.....or.....** and to subjects joined by **neither.....nor.....** . Here is a summary of it:

If **both parts are singular**, then the **verb** should be **singular** :
Either Fred or his wife is due to open the proceedings.   Neither praise nor punishment has any effect on him.
Nevertheless, in spoken English the plural is sometimes used.

If **both parts are plural**, or if just **one part is plural**, then the **verb** must be **plural**:
Either the walls or the pictures are at a strange angle.   Neither his enemies nor his friends trust him.
This sometimes gives an odd feeling to a sentence where a singular subject is put next to a clearly plural verb.
In such a case it is better to reorganize the sentence. Look at the next example to see what is involved.
Neither the buses nor the train were on time is better changed to: *Neither the train nor the buses were on time.*

More of a problem is created when **different persons** of the verb make up the subject. In such a case, the verb agrees with the person *nearest* to it: *Either my sister or I am responsible. We or he has to apologise.*
Once again, the best way out of it is to rewrite these odd sentences:
Either my sister is responsible, or I am. We have to apologise, or he has to.

Notice that **either**, by itself, should have a *singular* verb: *Was either of you responsible ?* Not: *Were either of you...*
However, in spoken English, the plural verb is now very common.
Neither also takes a singular verb: *Neither boy admits it, but neither of them is very honest.*
Both, by itself, has a *plural* verb: *Both of them were responsible.*

Also notice that we use *or instead of and* when two words or phrases are joined as the **object of a negative verb**:
I did not choose Jim or Fred. I chose Mary and Elizabeth instead.
When there are three items in such an object use a comma between the first two:
I do not want the trouble, the inconvenience or the aggravation.

Rule 179   Sentences may be simple, compound or complex

A **simple sentence** is a sentence that has only **one main verb**. Of course it may be a verb in several parts (i.e. a verb with several auxiliaries), but essentially there is only one piece of action. There is no second verb added to it in any way. There may well be a phrase added to it - or several phrases - but as you know a phrase does not have a verb of its own. So simple sentences can be quite long.

Here are some simple sentences according to this definition:

She has done her homework. After many protests she has done all the homework from last week.
Despite constantly complaining, I have still not been able to get her even to begin any of this week's homework.

A **compound sentence** has **two or more main verbs**, generally linked by *and* or *but*. In this kind of sentence the main verbs are equally important. In fact by taking away the conjunctions and inserting full stops and capital letters, two or more simple sentences could be used instead of the compound sentence.

Here are some examples:

She walked to the bus-stop, and caught a bus. He wrote to me often, but I never replied.
They chased the fox through the woods, but lost the scent at the stream, and could not pick it up again.
Go down past the shopping centre, turn right at the crossroads, and you'll see it in front of you.
Without a moment's thought he turned, still smiling in contempt at his enemies, sprang onto the broken bridge, and leapt down into the swirling flood of the river.

Notice that the last example has several participles used as adjectives - but these are not main verbs.

A **complex sentence** may have one main verb or several, but it also has **one or more subordinate clauses**. You have studied clauses in several of the earlier rules, so you know what they are.

Here are some examples:

There is the man that I was waiting for. The house, which is very old indeed, is rumoured to be haunted.
As you are standing up, could you fetch me that book. Send in the next applicant when you go out.
If you can spare the time, I should like to hear about it. Although he is my brother, he is a despicable creature.
When I had seem him, in order to make things quite clear, I noted down what he had said as carefully as I could on a single sheet of paper, which I then sent to Inspector Lestrade, who was already looking into the case.

The clauses used in complex sentences have many different types, and are essential to writing good English. It is better to use some complex sentences in your writing, rather than merely rely on simple or compound sentences. The best writing will always use a mixture of the three kinds of sentence.

Rule 180   Direct speech is indicated by speech marks

Direct speech is the name given to the **actual words** that are said, when these are stated in writing.

The **actual words** spoken must always be put inside **speech marks** (also known as **quotation marks** or **inverted commas**). Speech marks are small marks like commas above the line, which enclose the words spoken. In handwriting it is usual to use two inverted commas before and two after. The inverted commas at the start of the piece of speech face to the right, those at the end face to the left. In typewriting and printing either a single ('.........') or a double ("........") set of inverted commas may be used. (These often have no 'direction'.)

We usually state the person saying the words in direct speech immediately after the words themselves, separated from them by a comma. There is no comma if the direct speech ends with a question mark or exclamation mark. We do not put full stops after pieces of direct speech when they are followed by a comma plus a verb of speaking. The comma always goes inside the speech marks.

So: *"Come in," said Mr Bennett. "I can see you," called Mandy.*
"You're very quiet in there," said the teacher. "What do you want?" I asked. "Stop it!" shouted their mother.

Notice that where the person speaking is indicated by a **noun**, we generally reverse the order of subject and verb, and write it as **verb plus subject**. It used to be common to reverse the order with pronouns too, but now we generally keep the normal order with pronouns. So: *"Come in!" he said*, is more usual than *"Come in!" said he*. However: *"Come in," Mr Bennett said* sounds rather odd. *"Come in, " said Mr Bennett* is better.

We sometimes put the speaker in the middle of what is spoken. This can be done at the end of one sentence of direct speech and before the next - which will then carry straight on (inside its speech marks), without needing a new verb of speaking. Sometimes it is done by putting the speaker right in the middle of a sentence.
Look at these examples:
"I'm very pleased to see you," he said. "Do come in. Pull up a chair, and I'll get you a warm drink."
"Do you wish to see me now," he asked, "or could you come up in half an hour or so ?"
Notice in the first example that the inverted commas start again after *he said*, but we do not need to repeat the words *he said* for the new speech: it is obvious who said them.
In the second example, we have to separate the words of speaking (*he asked*) from the words spoken not only by ending the speech marks before, and starting them again when the speech starts again; but also by a pair of ordinary commas. The thing to remember is: **put spoken words and spoken words only inside speech marks**. Also in the second example, notice that the question mark has to wait till the end of the sentence - even though the words of speaking are in the middle.

When you begin a piece of direct speech for the first time, or when **someone new starts speaking**, or when the speaker changes, it is usual to **start a new paragraph**. This means start a new line. In handwriting, we generally go a few spaces in from the edge when starting a new paragraph. In typing and printing this is not always done. Here is an example of a piece of dialogue (conversation):
"I have often wondered," said Sexton Quake, puffing sagaciously at his smoky old pipe," whatever happened to Professor Sorriarty. Have you heard anything about him ?"
"He was killed by Sherlock Domes, wasn't he?" inquired young Tom Tiddles, the intrepid detective's youthful associate. "Or was it the other way round ?" he muttered to himself.
"Well he would be over a hundred by now, " added fellow detective, Miss Marbles. " Can I pour you another cup of tea, Mr Quake ?"
"No thank you, but I will have a scone."
"I'll have two," agreed Tom Tiddles, and added, "Ow!" as his boss slapped his outstretched hand with a magnifying glass. "That doesn't happen to other detectives."
"Gentlemen, stop! I fear you may be eating the evidence," cried Miss Marbles.

Notice how the division into paragraphs does make it possible to tell who is talking, even when it is not stated. It is even possible to include one short piece of speech in a paragraph of its own with no mention of who says it - because it is clear from the context (the surroundings).
Also notice how the use of **different words** of speaking in place of *said* makes things more interesting.

It is possible to put the verb of speaking before the piece of direct speech, but this can cause problems because you then have to start a new speech paragraph at once. The best thing to do is use a **colon** (two dots, one above the other) after the verb of speaking and then go onto the next line for the actual words:
He turned to me and said:
"I'm sorry, Joe, but you know too much."

Very small pieces of direct speech, in the middle of a great deal of other material, can simply be included without a paragraph of their own. However, in this case it is best to use indirect speech - as explained in the following rule.

Rule 181   Indirect speech does not use the actual words spoken

Indirect speech keeps the **meaning** of what was said, but does **not** keep the **original words**.
Since it does not give the original words it has **no speech marks**.

A **statement** in direct speech is turned into an **indirect statement**.
Indirect statements are generally introduced by a verb of speaking followed by **that**:
He said that he was ready. You told me that you were coming. I replied that I was unable to be there.
He says that we have lost at home again. You told me that you had never been abroad.
Her answer was that it would be quite impossible. Jenks claims that he never left the room.
Notice that we do **not** say: *spoke that*....
You are already familiar with something very similar following verbs like *know, think, see* etc:
*I **believe that** he is guilty. I had **hoped that** it was not true. The staff **feared that** the firm would close down.*
*Did you **notice that** we were both reading the same book. She **pretended that** the picture was genuine.*
We do sometimes **miss out** *that* in indirect statements: *You said you would. He admitted [that] it was true.*

A **question** in direct speech is turned into an **indirect question**.
Indirect questions are introduced by a verb of asking followed by **whether** or **if**:
She asked if we had any cheese. Mrs Simpson was asking whether Edward would be there.
I have inquired several times whether a day return is available.
Indirect questions can also be introduced by an **original question word**, if there was one:
I asked him where he had been and what he had done. He asked us who was responsible.
She was asking why all the lights had been left on.
Once again similar clauses follow verbs of *knowing* etc: *They wanted to **know whether** we were going.*
*I **wonder if** anyone's in. Have you **decided where** to go this year ? I can **guess what** you've been up to, my lad.*

A **command** in direct speech becomes an **indirect command**.
Indirect commands are introduced by a verb of ordering plus **the infinitive**:
He told them to get on with their work. The inspector ordered everyone to keep perfectly still.
Since we do not use 'said to' in English, original verbs of saying need to become **tell** or **order** to introduce indirect
commands. So: *"Stop it, boy!"said the teacher* has to become: *The teacher told the boy to stop it.*

It is quite possible to use indirect speech and direct speech together, but try not to change from one to the other
very often. If there is a good deal of dialogue, direct speech is better. In formal letters or essays, where there is not
much speech, the indirect form is better. If a piece of speech is being reported inside another piece of speech, it
often makes more sense to do the reporting in the indirect form:
"Are you the fellow who was asking if Mr Marrowfat was here ?" inquired the clerk.

The **titles** of books, films, plays etc. are often put in quotation marks.
Also inside quotation marks are actual **quotations** - pieces taken from a work written by someone else,
and stated in the original words:
"Doesn't 'Water, water everywhere' come from Coleridge's 'Rime of the Ancient Mariner'?" he asked.
Notice in this example how single inverted commas are used for the quotation and the title, but double inverted
commas for the main piece of speech. When you have two different uses of inverted commas together like this,
it is sensible to use the two different types that are available.

In printing, titles and sometimes quotations are shown in *italic type*. Do **not** try to do this in handwriting.

Rule 182 Some words need to be altered in indirect speech

The main **alterations** needed (apart from to the *verbs*) in **indirect speech** are to the **pronouns**.
Personal pronouns in reported speech that refer back to a speaker in the third person must themselves become third person. This difficult rule is best understood by some examples:
"I am ready," he said becomes in indirect speech: *He said that he was ready.* If you think about it, it has to change in this way, because: *He said that I was ready* would mean something completely different.
"Are you ready?" she asked could become either of two possible alternatives.
One is: *She asked him if he was ready.* If the person being spoken to (**you**) is still around, however, we might want to make the indirect speech: *She asked you whether you were ready.*

Very often in reported speech we want to change whole passages from first person (*I* or *we*) to third person (*he, she* or *they*). So the main verb may also move from *I said* to *he said*:
"My house is the one at the end," I said could become: *He said that his house was the one at the end.*

As you may have noticed in the above example, *possessive adjectives* and *possessive pronouns* will also need to change when the personal pronouns change. So *my* will become *his* or *her*, and *mine* will become *his* or *hers*.
Our will become *their*, and *ours* will become *theirs*.

Other changes appear in the time scale. When we use **direct speech** everything is **here and now**.
In **indirect speech** it becomes **there and then**. So *here* becomes *there*; *this* becomes *that*; *these* become *those*; *today*, *tomorrow* and *yesterday* become *that day, the following day* and *the previous day*.
These changes do not always need to be made. They are most likely to be needed if the verb of speaking is in a past tense, and the events reported are already in past time. Only make the changes that make sense:
"I saw you yesterday," I said might become: *I said that I had seen him the previous day.*
"Meet me here this afternoon, Jimmy," I said might become: *He told Jimmy to meet him there that afternoon.*

In indirect speech we sometimes need to **insert who is being spoken to**:
"Stop it at once!" he said becomes: *He told **them** to stop it at once.*
Without *them* the indirect command does not work.

The main change from direct to indirect speech is, however, in the tense of the verb, and that is explained in the following rule.

Rule 183 The sequence of tenses governs verbs in indirect speech

When you put something into indirect speech what you are doing is taking it one stage further away - or one step further into the past. The **tense** of the verb in the indirect speech is **controlled by** the tense of the verb of speaking **introducing** the indirect speech.

If the verb of speaking is **present or future**, the verb in the reported speech can be **any tense**: past, present or future, depending on which is closest to the original speech and makes most sense.
He says that he will go tomorrow. He says that he is going in a minute. He says that he went yesterday.
He says that he had been once, but hasn't been lately. He says that he will have been by this time next week.

Rule 183 cont.

If the verb of speaking is in one of the several past tenses, things are rather more complicated.
Past tenses for this purpose come in two categories.

Firstly, if the verb of speaking is in the **perfect** (or *future perfect*) tense, the verb in the indirect speech can,
once again be in **any tense**, preferably the one closest to the sense of the original:
He has said that he will go tomorrow. He has said that he is going now. He has said that he has gone before.

Secondly, if the verb is in the **past (simple)** tense, the **past continuous (imperfect)**, or the **pluperfect**,
then the verb in the indirect speech has to be changed. All the following sections are about this particular case.

An **original present** tense becomes **past**:
"I am working hard,"she said becomes: *She said that she was working hard.*
"I work hard," she said becomes: *She said that she worked hard.*

An **original past** tense becomes **pluperfect**:
"I was working hard,"she said becomes: *She said that she had been working hard.*
"I worked hard,"she said becomes: *She said that she had worked hard.*
"I have worked hard," she said becomes: *She said that she had worked hard.*

However, we do not like too much of the pluperfect tense in English, so the rule is quite often broken,
and we simply use a past tense: *She said that she worked hard* etc.
Alternatively, the pluperfect is used, but only in the abbreviated form: *She said that she'd worked hard.*

For an **original future** tense in direct speech *change* will and shall *to* would in indirect speech:
"I shall work hard," she said becomes: *She said that she would work hard.*

Notice that even when *I* or *we* are used in indirect speech, *would* is nearly always used instead of *should*, because
should has the more common meaning of *ought to*:
I said that I would work hard rather than: *I said that I should work hard*, which means something rather different.

The modal verbs *can* and *may* also change. **Can** *becomes* **could** and **may** *becomes* **might**:
"I may go tomorrow," he said becomes: *He said that he might go on the following day.*
"I can work hard if I want to," she said becomes: *She said that she could work hard if she wanted to.*

The rule of the sequence of tenses applies in exactly the same way in **other clauses** introduced by **that**, and **if** and
whether - in fact in all clauses that are like indirect statement and indirect questions in their form. For example:
It surprised me (past) *that he had written* (pluperfect).
I was wondering (past) *whether you would come* (future with *would*, not *will*).
I never forgave him (past) *for what he had done* (pluperfect).

Remember that the complications of the **sequence of tenses** *only* happen after a **main verb in the past**,
past continuous, or **pluperfect** tenses. Unfortunately we very often introduce indirect speech with a verb in the
past tense. When we do, the verb in the indirect speech should very probably go in the pluperfect tense (with *had*)
though a past or imperfect may also be correct. Similarly, *will* becomes *would* etc.

Rule 184   The subjunctive is still occasionally used in English

There is still one form of the verb we have not yet considered. This is known as the subjunctive.
The **subjunctive** is used for expressing **wishes**, and some **conditions**, and in some **indirect speech**.

In those cases where the subjunctive is used it has two main variations from the ordinary verb
(which is correctly called 'the indicative').
In the **present tense** of any verb, the **third person singular** has **no s**; so we would write:
he go, she like etc. instead of *he goes* and *she likes*.
In the **present tense** of the verb **to be**, **be** is used for **all persons**. So we would write:
I be, you be, he be, we be, they be.
In the **past tense were** is used for **all persons**. So we would write:
I were, he were etc. instead of *I was, he was* etc.
These changes apply when the verb **to be** is used as an **auxiliary verb** as well.

We shall now look at some examples of the uses of this strange form.
The **subjunctive** is used in some **wishes** or **requests**:
God bless you! Devil take it! Long live the king! Come what may! So be it! Be it known that....
None of these look quite so odd when you think that they are very like the **imperative**, which we constantly use to
make rather similar requests. Also the list of examples given here contains many of the common expressions
where a subjunctive is actually used for a wish or request.
We often use **let** or occasionally **may** as an auxiliary to say the same sort of thing:
Let the villain live then! Let them come in. May you all do well in your exams.

The **subjunctive** is used in some **conditional** sentences with **if**.
As you may remember (and if you don't you should look back to *Rule 174*), one type of conditional clause is the
unreal or **impossible**, when the condition expressed is not true - and very probably could not be true.
In this sort of conditional we do sometimes use a subjunctive, to stress the unreality:
If he were alive now he would be nearly seventy. (There is nothing wrong with: *If he was alive* - but *were*
is better.)
If he come, then I shall slay him. (*Come* instead of *comes* is the subjunctive used to suggest that the condition
is not expected to be fulfilled. Even so, since it is set in future time, it could happen, and so the subjunctive
sounds odd.)
Very often we cannot tell if a subjunctive is being used, since it is frequently the same as the indicative:
*If they were alive now.....*could be either; *If I come.....*could also be either.
Notice: *Were he to go, then I would go with him*, where **were he to go** means: **if he were to go**.

If only may be used to express a **wish**, and is sometimes also followed by the **subjunctive** - when the wish is an
impossible one: *If only I were there! If only she were not dead.*
Similar, but now rather old fashioned, is **would that**: *Would that I were there! Would that she were alive.*
Since the subjunctive is used for wishing, as you might expect it is sometimes found after **verbs of wishing**:
I wished that it were so! I wish I were there!
The **subjunctive** is used after **though**, **although** and **even if** in the same way:
Though he die, his spirit lives on. Even if I were rich, I would still live in my little council house.

The **subjunctive** occasionally appears in **indirect speech** after verbs of **requesting**:
He moved that the House adjourn. He suggested that it be recorded in the minutes.
It was requested that she leave the room during the voting. I move that the amendment be now put.
We very often insert **should** in this sort of sentence: *He suggested that it should be recorded in the minutes.*

Rule 185   Full stops, question marks and exclamation marks are used to end sentences

If what you have written is not a sentence, do not end it with one of these marks (except in one or two special cases mentioned in some of the following rules). Remember that a sentence must make sense by itself. However, even a very short group of words can make sense in a particular context (i.e. in particular surroundings).

So one- or two-word imperatives, which have simple full stops or exclamation marks are generally perfectly good sentences: *Stop! Come here!*

Other things we exclaim, or say aloud generally, often appear as sentences, particularly when we are writing passages of direct speech: *Well I never. Fancy that. Oh dear!*

Questions can also be very short, provided that they make sense: *She hasn't, has she ?   Did he ?   Why?*
One word answers to questions are also sentences in themselves: *Can I have one ? No.   Surrender, dogs! Never!*

In fact, many sentences that break the rules in direct speech still count as sentences, because they are the actual words said. In your own writing, try not to break the rule that a sentence must make sense in itself (except in pieces of dialogue). In narrative (stories), descriptive, and factual writing, use correctly formed sentences.

Rule 186   The question mark is used for direct not indirect questions

This rule is to reinforce what you should already know. When questions are put in the form: *He asked if*.......
She wanted to know whether......   *I inquired when*......   then there are no inverted commas, because the speech is indirect. The actual words are not used, nor is a question mark used.
When you are writing speech, always ask yourself whether it is direct or indirect. If it is **direct** you will be using **speech marks**, and the questions will need **question marks**. In fact you will probably find it easy to remember to put in the question marks; so use them as a reminder to put in the speech marks as well.

Sometimes you may want to ask a question in the middle of a piece of writing that is not asked by a character, but by you as the writer. It will not need speech marks, but it will need a question mark if you ask it directly.

Statements can be made into questions by inserting a question mark after them. When we <u>say</u> this sort of question we show that it is not just a statement by changing the tone of our voice. So: *You are joining us tonight, Cedric ?*
Imperatives can be turned into questions in exactly the same way: *"Stop it ? What do you mean, 'Stop it'?"*

On the other hand, some questions of the sort that we ask by tacking a question onto the end of a statement (See *Rules 105*), or by answering a statement with a question, are not really questions at all:
He never did that, did he ? Did he really ?   Well, would you believe it !
All of these three examples have the form of questions. Since the first two could at least get an answer (even if only 'yes'), they have been given question marks here. The last one is an expression commonly used just to express surprise, so it has been given an exclamation mark here. Whether an answer is at all likely is the best way to decide.

A question mark inside brackets (?) is sometimes used to indicate that what has just been said is possibly wrong or at least open to doubt. In factual writing you can do this, if you really need to. Do not do it to suggest that you are unsure of your own facts or opinions.

Rule 187   The exclamation mark is used for exclamations

This sounds very obvious, but is here as a rule for a reason. It is very easy to use exclamation marks a great deal, to draw attention to a particular sentence you have written. That is a perfectly acceptable and correct use of the exclamation mark. Its purpose is to **draw attention**. However, it is advisable not to use it in this way until your English is very good. Otherwise you will tend to use it far too often, and your writing will be powdered with exclamation marks. If you really must use it in this way, ration yourself to one per piece of writing.

Some people use an exclamation mark in brackets after a word or phrase to draw attention to it.
This is not wrong, but people who mark English exams still do not like it.
Double, or treble exclamation marks, as in: *Wow!!!* are a very bad idea. They make your writing look juvenile.

Rule 188   Capital letters have several uses

You already know most of the uses of capital letters. This rule groups them together to help you remember them.

A capital must be used to **start a sentence**. This is true for one word sentences as well as for others.
It is also true for sentences inside sentences, which can happen when you insert something in brackets:
After the battle (It had been a particularly fierce engagement.) the dead lay piled in heaps.

A capital must be used to begin each **new piece of direct speech**, and each new sentence within direct speech.
So: *"Hurry!" he said. "We must go. There is no time to lose."*
However, where the words said continue a sentence interrupted by the word of saying, there is no capital:
"You need not know," he added in a whisper," who I am, or where we are going. Just follow me."

A capital must be used for a **proper noun** - a name.
Check back to *Rule 15* about this, and notice that prepositions and conjunctions inside names do not generally get capitals, but all other words in the name do.
Names include **official titles**, and also forms of address like **Mr** and **Dr** and **initials**.
So: *the Houses of Parliament, New York City, Connaught Circus, Lord Krishna, St Nicholas, Santa Claus, the Marquis of Queensberry, the United States, Sri Lanka, the Pacific Ocean, the Thames, the Snowy Mountains, William Shakespeare, Mr Dickens, Dr Crippen, the Titanic, the Trades Union Congress, Oriflamme Publishing.*
A capital should be used when a **particular title or name** is used to refer to a specific holder of that title:
Of all the pyramids, the Great Pyramid is the most spectacular. Gentlemen, the toast is: the Queen!
The assembled heads of state fell silent as the President entered.
Notice that **God** and the gods and holy books of all religions must have capital letters.

Adjectives formed from proper nouns must also keep their capitals:
English, Pakistani, Dutch, Madrasi, Glaswegian, Shakespearian, Platonic, Carthusian.
Many but not all of these proper adjectives also have common use as nouns (generally with one of the articles).
The personal pronoun **I** is always a capital.
Each new line of **poetry** begins with a capital.

Capitals are very often used throughout in **signs** and notices. When they are not, you occasionally see them used to start every word. This is not particularly logical. Since the object of a notice is to call attention to itself, the best plan is to use capitals throughout if it is short, and to use ordinary punctuation if it is rather longer.
Writing whole words in capitals as a way of stressing them in ordinary writing is done by some writers, but is not a particularly good idea. See *Rule 198* below about stress by means of underlining and italics.

Rule 189   Commas are used to indicate pauses within sentences

If a full stop indicates just what it says - a stop, then a **comma** indicates a **pause**. Wherever there is a natural break in a sentence, it is often sensible to mark it with a comma. Commas make your writing easier to read, by breaking it up into manageable chunks. When you are reading a piece of writing, the commas tell you where the breaks are. Particularly if reading aloud, pause at those commas which break up the sentence into its constituent parts.

So commas are used to mark the end of clauses, and sometimes of longer phrases. In this way they give structure to longer sentences. Do not use them when they are not needed. Only use one to separate the two halves of a compound sentence joined by *and* (See *Rule 179*) if you need to. Make sure they go in the right place and do not scatter them too freely. Too many commas are as confusing as too few.
The simple rule is: **Use a comma when a pause or break is *necessary*.**

Do not use a comma where a full stop is required. A comma cannot join two separate sentences.
So: *We went to the park, we played football there* is incorrect. Either replace the comma with *and*, or change it to a full stop and begin a new sentence: *We went to the park. We played football there.*
Notice that if we **do not repeat the pronoun**, and insert an adverb like *then*, the comma is correct: *He saw me, then ran away* is correct; so is: *He saw me and then he ran away*, and: *He saw me and ran away.*
However: *He saw me, then he ran away* is not quite correct.

Commas are also used **to separate words**. This may happen when there are several adjectives together describing one noun, or even several adverbs modifying one verb. Do not insert a comma when you have two words joined by a conjunction. Do insert a comma when you have two words not joined by a conjunction. When there are three words linked together, generally the first and second are separated by a comma, and the second and third are joined by *and*. When *and* is included we often leave out the comma in front of it. Sometimes the conjunction is omitted, and just commas are used. Demonstrative adjectives (*this, that, these, those*) and numbers are treated as if they were articles, and are never separated from other adjectives following them by a comma.
Here are some examples:
a red and green dress; the red, white and blue of the flag; this sudden, unexpected change;
a long, cool, welcome drink; It made the kill swiftly, silently and efficiently.
Do not put a comma between adjectives when the first is modifying the meaning of the second:
A bright blue dress means a dress which is bright blue;
A bright, blue dress means a dress which is not only bright but also blue.

When writing **lists**, each item is followed by a comma, until the last two which are linked by *and* (with or without a comma). However, occasionally you have lists where there is a linked pair counting as one item. This example will show you how this is done: *Remember to bring your knife and fork, wellingtons and snow-shoes, emergency rations and warning flares, tents, tent-pegs and guy-ropes.*

When writing **long numbers** in figures, a comma is inserted after every three figures - starting at the right:
seven thousand - 7,000; one hundred and one thousand and one - 101,001;
seven million, three hundred and twenty-seven thousand, nine hundred and ninety-nine - 7,327,999.
Notice how the commas also help to break up the number when it is written out in words.

Introductory words or phrases are followed by a comma:
Nevertheless, I do not agree. Despite everything, I still do not agree!
Words like *however* often appear as the second word, or even later in the new sentence. When this is done they must have a comma on each side: *Queen Victoria, however, was not amused.*

Commas at the beginning and end of a phrase or clause separate it out from the rest of the sentence. Only shut a phrase or clause off with double commas if the rest of the sentence really can manage without it. For example:

He arrived, even though I had asked him to come in the evening, on the noon train.
I am prepared, under the circumstances, and with some reservations, to forget the whole matter.
In my opinion, whatever that Mrs Molotov may say, our Sharon was still, on the whole, the best of the bunch.
Do not separate the subject from the verb with a comma - even when the subject is long and complicated:
The comma in: *The arrangements we have made for electing the new members to the standing committee of the society dealing with the celebrations,* come into force next week is wrong.

Be careful with **relative clauses** (See *Rules 164* and *165*).
If the relative clause is a **defining** one (often introduced by *that*) it is not separated out by commas:
Do you remember the little town that we visited in Normandy ?   She's the one that I saw there.
If the relative clause is **descriptive**, it generally is separated out by commas:
That fellow, whom you seem to like so much, is no better than a common criminal.
This proposal, which I do not support, is full of contradictions.
Phrases in **apposition** (See *Rule 166*) are usually separated out by commas:
Mr Sawyer, our newly-elected leader, is already under pressure from rival factions.
Names of people spoken to are also separated out by commas:
Is that you, Fred ?   Do you, Sarah Blenkinsop, take this man as your lawful wedded husband ?

Questions attached to the end of sentences (to form loaded questions: see *Rule 108*) are always separated from the rest of the sentence by a comma: *You are playing, aren't you ? You didn't do it, did you, Joe ?*
Yes and no as answers to questions usually come first, and are followed by a comma. If for some reason they are put in the middle of a sentence they require commas on each side:
Yes, we have no bananas. No, there aren't any. Well, yes, I suppose so.

Rule 190   The semicolon indicates a longer pause

The semicolon (a comma with a dot written above it - **;**) is used to show a pause which is longer or more important than that for which you would use a comma, but not sufficiently definite for you to use a full stop.

Semicolons are particularly useful in long or complicated **lists**, especially when some items in the list already have commas within themselves. This happens in lists involving phrases rather than just words. The semicolon is also useful in lists which include different types of things, or lists where there are several items in one category followed by several items in another. The items are then separated by commas; the two categories are separated by the semicolon. Here are two examples of the use of the semicolon in lists:
The following are the winners: John, Robert, Bill; Mary, Susan and Tabitha.
I'd like eggs, bacon, chips and tomatoes twice; sausage and mash once; and three teas.

The semicolon can also be used to put two **clauses** together, when you want to link them for comparison or contrast, but do not want to employ any particular conjunction. In effect you are linking two separate sentences when you do this. It should not be done with a comma; it can be done with a semicolon. For example:
He is a brave man without any doubt; some might say he is rash.
The situation is intolerable: we are not at peace; we are not at war; we are merely at a loss.
In **complex sentences** with several clauses, the semicolon may help to give a clearer break than a comma:
Although he has spoken in favour of this, I am unsure of his motives, which, in the past have not been above question; nor, for that reason, can I wholeheartedly give my support to the cause he now champions.

Rule 191   The colon is primarily used for introducing lists

The colon (one stop placed above another - **:**) is used for introducing something that is to follow. Its main use is in introducing a list, either of words or of phrases; but it can also be used to introduce the second half of a sentence which follows on from the first half; and to introduce direct speech, when the words of speaking come before the words spoken. (In this last case it is better to use a colon than a comma.) Here are examples of each:
Please hand in the following: pens, pencils and rulers; your diagrams; and last night's homework.
Do not end a sentence with a preposition: a preposition is the wrong thing to end a sentence up with.
After a long silence he replied:
"It's too late. There is no escape...."
As you will have noticed in this book, the colon is also used to introduce examples.

Rule 192   The dash is mainly used to add extra information

It is best not to use the dash very much; it is rather a casual piece of punctuation. In fact its main use is to tack on an **afterthought**: *He's in his room - third door on the right. Let me know if you're coming - and when.*
The dash can be used to introduce a **change of direction** within a sentence, when you are making a contrast or comparison, or stating a condition: *He's a big fellow, certainly - not very fast, though.*

A dash always **separates** what follows it from the rest of the sentence, and a phrase or clause with a dash at each end is completely separated out. A pair of commas has the same effect, but rather less decisively. For example:
The house at the far end - the one with the overgrown garden - is where we think they're hiding.
A pair of brackets (See the next rule.) is better than a pair of dashes.
You can use a dash to **introduce a list**, but a colon is better. You can also use a colon followed by a dash.

All these uses work best in direct speech and in informal writing, but not in formal letters, essays, or documents.

Rule 193   Brackets are used to separate off pieces of writing

Brackets are always used in pairs, one bracket before and the other after.
You may put brackets round a single word, a phrase, a clause, a sentence or a whole paragraph.
The effect of the brackets is to take everything inside them out of the main stream of your writing.
There are various reasons you may want to do this. The contents of brackets often add extra bits of information or explanation that are not essential but may be helpful. Make sure that what is inside the brackets makes sense by itself, and what is outside the brackets makes sense without needing what is inside.
Brackets are a much stronger device for separating pieces of writing that commas or dashes.
So: *Tickets may be purchased (price ten pounds) from Grabbit and Runne Ltd.*
The whole school was duly assembled. (This was most unusual.) The Principal himself made the announcement.

If you put a whole sentence in brackets, its full stop also belongs inside the brackets. If something in brackets merely happens to occur at the end of a longer sentence, the full stop belongs outside the brackets.

There are various shapes for brackets, the most common being round **( )** and square **[ ]**. If you really need to put something in brackets which is within a passage already in brackets you may use the alternative shape.
Otherwise, stick to one or the other in any one piece of writing.
Square brackets do tend to be used for adding very short pieces of extra information.
Round brackets are often put round reference numbers or letters - particularly in lists of questions: *(1) (a).*

Rule 194   Inverted commas have various uses

Direct speech consists of the **exact words used by the speaker**. All direct speech must be surrounded by **quotation marks**, also known as **speech marks** or **inverted commas**. You should already know this from *Rule 180*.

You should also know that inverted commas are a pair of **commas above the line**. At the beginning of a piece of speech these marks face towards the right. At the end they face towards the left.

This rule is to remind you about the use of inverted commas in direct speech, add some further information about how to punctuate properly when using inverted commas, and also to give some of their additional uses.

Sometimes only a **single** inverted comma is used instead of a pair. There must still be one at the beginning and one at the end of the piece of speech of course.

In your writing it is best to save the single inverted commas for use when you have a piece of speech inside another piece of speech.

Inverted commas are also often put around the **titles** of books, plays etc. Sometimes titles of books are underlined instead of being put inside quotation marks. In printing, it is usual to put titles etc. in italics: *slanted writing like this*. Do not try to do this with your handwriting, however.

Inverted commas should be put round **quotations**. A quotation is something said or written by another person that you repeat in your own writing. You only use quotation marks if you are stating the exact original words.
So: *As Shakespeare put it: "Brutus is an honourable man."*

Sometimes **foreign words** are put in quotation marks when they are used in English.

Quotation marks can also be used to mark a particular word or phrase as **sarcastic** or ironic. This means you are using it with a different meaning, often the opposite of its usual meaning.
For example: *Brutus is an 'honourable' man.*
In most cases it should be clear that you are being ironic without needing quotation marks.

Punctuation associated with pieces of **direct speech** inside quotation marks also goes inside the quotation marks. Remember not to use a full stop at the end of a piece of speech if a word of speaking follows.
You can use a question mark or exclamation mark in this way, however. For example:
"Come on! What are you waiting for ?" he shouted.
"We're almost ready," I replied. "Just give us another minute."

When a word of speaking is sandwiched in the middle of a continuing piece of direct speech it is followed by a comma (which comes before the inverted commas re-start):
"Do you want to come in," he said, "or are you going to stand out there all night ?"

Be careful that pieces of punctuation that are not part of the direct speech are not included within the quotation marks. For example: *Do you know who wrote: "Brutus is an honourable man"?*
Here the question mark is not part of the quotation and therefore belongs outside the quotation marks.

Also notice these examples which show the correct placing of the punctuation marks:
"He said, 'It wasn't me, sir', but I didn't believe him," I replied.
"I'm sure I heard him," I answered. "I thought he said, 'Come in'."

Rule 195 Paragraphs are used to divide pieces of writing into sections

In handwriting a **paragraph** is generally shown by starting its first sentence a little further in from the left hand margin (indenting). In printing and typing, a space is often left between paragraphs instead of indenting.

Paragraphs should generally each be about much the **same topic** or item. The next paragraph should start when you come to a natural break, or a change of topic. In long essays or compositions, and in letters, it is essential to break up what you are writing into readable chunks in this way. If you are planning a piece of writing in advance it often helps to work out a series of paragraph headings to help you get things into a sensible and logical order. There is no rule that says all paragraphs must be the same length.

Remember that every **new speaker** or change of speaker requires a new paragraph when you are writing in direct speech (with inverted commas). You can break this rule if only a few words of direct speech are included in a much longer piece of writing. In dialogue (frequent changes of speaker) it is essential.

Rule 196 The apostrophe is used for the possessive and for shortened forms

You already know the two uses of the **apostrophe**, so this is a rule for revision.
Firstly the apostrophe is used to form the **possessive** of nouns.
If the noun is **singular** you form the possessive by adding an **apostrophe** followed by the letter **s**.
If the noun is **plural**, and its plural form already **ends in s**, you put an **apostrophe after** the **s**.
If the noun is **plural** but its plural form does **not** end **in s**, add **apostrophe s**.
For example: *the man's opinion (one opinion of one man)*
                the girl's dolls (several dolls of one girl)
                the girls' dolls (several dolls of several girls)
                the men's opinion (one opinion of several men)
                the men's opinions (several opinions of several men)
Put the **apostrophe s** on the **owner, not** on the item that is **owned.**

Do not use an apostrophe to form normal plurals.
"Apple's, pear's and banana's for sale" is utter nonsense.

An apostrophe is also used to indicate the place where one or more **letters** have been **left out** in a word that has been shortened. Most of these are the shortened forms of verbs with pronouns, and verbs with negatives:
you've, he's, they'd, we'll, I'm; don't, mustn't, can't, shan't.

Learn the difference between these:

its meaning *of it*, or *belonging to it* - no apostrophe
it's meaning *it is* or *it has* - apostrophe

there meaning *that place*, or as in '*there is*' etc. - no apostrophe
their meaning *of them* (adjective) - no apostrophe
they're meaning *they are* - apostrophe
theirs meaning *of them* (pronoun) - no apostrophe
there's meaning *there is* or *there has* - apostrophe.

Rule 197 A hyphen indicates a link between words or parts of words

A hyphen is a rather short dash (-).
It is used when two words are **linked together** to form a kind of compound word. There is often a good deal of doubt as to whether two commonly linked words need the link indicated by a hyphen. Check back to *Rule 40*.
Notice its use in phrases where an adjective with modifying adverb are used to describe a noun:
a well-known landmark; a happily-married man. Do not link other adjectives and adverbs with a hyphen.

We quite often put a hyphen in a word where **two vowels** that are said separately come next to each other.
The two commonest are: *co-operate* and *no-one.* We use the hyphen when putting a prefix in front of a 'proper adjective' (the sort with a capital letter): *anti-German.*

A hyphen can sometimes help to prevent confusion. There is a difference between: *We shall reform the society* and *We shall re-form the society.* (*Reform* means 'change'; *re-form* means 'start again'.)

A hyphen is also used to indicate that a word **continues** on the next line, when you run out of space, and have to break the word into two pieces. If you have to do this, try to break the word in a natural place (between two syllables). It used to be a rule that the second half of the word should always begin with a consonant. This is less important than breaking it in a natural place.

Rule 198 Other punctuation marks are sometimes used

Accents are used on foreign words where they belong. If you are not sure whether or not to use one, or where it goes, or even what it looks like, simply leave it off. In fact only include an accent if you are sure about it.

The **asterisk** (*) is used to mark a piece of text about which there is a footnote. Other curious marks are also used for this, as are tiny numbers written above the line. Try not to put footnotes in your own writing (unless you are writing a work of scholarship of course), but if you do, indicate what they refer to with an asterisk.

You can use a kind of pointer (which may have various shapes) to insert a word or words you have missed out.

If you want to cross something out, do it with a single straight line through it; if there is more than one word to be crossed out it is sensible to use a ruler.

You should recognise the signs for pounds (£) and for dollars ($).
% is the per cent sign. **@** is used to mean *at* when you want to state a price: *three books @ £4.25*
& is known as the ampersand. It simply means *and*.
Learn how to do it, as it is very useful in writing notes, but do not use it in formal writing.

There are many other signs in maths and science, but they are not strictly punctuation marks.

In things that are printed you will often come across italics and bold type.
Italics means slanted printing *like this*.   Bold type means heavy printing **like this**.
They are used to mark something as different from the rest of the text.
In handwriting, you can use <u>underlining</u> in their place.
When you are giving a title to a piece of work always underline it.
Read *Rule 194* on inverted commas again for their use to mark certain things.

Rule 199   Abbreviations are shortened forms of words

You already know one kind of abbreviation - where letters missed out are indicated by an **apostrophe**.

Apart from these particular examples that you have learnt, other abbreviations do not have apostrophes. Instead they very often end with a full stop. If the abbreviation ends with the last letter of the word being abbreviated, it is quite correct to miss out the stop. Other abbreviations should have a full stop, but in modern usage the stop is very often left out, especially for common abbreviations.
If you are not sure, <u>do</u> put the stop in; it is never wrong to do so.
If an abbreviation is followed by a comma, it is best to include the full stop, even for words where it is now usual to miss it out. So *St* standing for street can be written without a full stop, but where a comma follows it (in an address for example), then the full stop should be included.
Mr, *Mrs* and *Dr* are now nearly always written without a stop.
Abbreviations are often very much shorter than the words they stand for.
Co. stands for company; *Ltd.* stands for limited; *recd.* stands for received, *info.* stands for information, and so on.
Some abbreviations are just the first letters of words: *c.o.d.* for example is *cash on delivery.*

Abbreviations made up of the initials of words are very commonly used for proper names, especially when these are long and cumbersome. It is much easier to say *TUC* than *Trades Union Congress*.
Abbreviations consisting entirely of capital letters are very often written without any full stops.
You should use capital letters in abbreviations if the original words had capital letters.
Sometimes the letters of the abbreviation form a kind of word by themselves (pronounced as if it was an ordinary word). So when we use *GATT* for the *General Agreement on Tariffs and Trade*, we pronounce it 'gat'. This sort of word is called an acronym. It should still be written with capital letters, but sometimes is not. There is generally no spacing between the letters, and the full stops after the letters are now nearly always left out.
If an abbreviation ends a sentence give it a single full stop - not two.

Rule 200   Some foreign words and their abbreviations are used in English

We do use some foreign words and expressions in English. Most of the words in the language have in fact come into it from other languages. However, newly arrived words are often shown in printing by the use of italics, and in handwriting by their inclusion inside inverted commas.
So we may speak of *sang froid* (meaning coolness in the face of difficulties) - from French; and *angst* (a sort of general anxiety) - from German.
Latin and Greek words are used as technical terms in science and medicine.
There are also various legal terms. Probably the best known is: *Habeas corpus* (meaning something like: *There must be some evidence*, and the name of a procedure to prevent people being kept in prison without a hearing).

Much more important are the abbreviations of one or two foreign words:
The commonest is probably *etc.* which is short for *etcetera* (from Latin, and meaning *and the rest*).
Two other common examples are abbreviations using the first letters of words:
i.e. is short for *id est*, Latin for *that is*, and you use it when explaining something;
e.g. is short for *exempli gratia*, Latin for *for example* - and you use it to state an example.
Try not to mix these two up.
Also remember: *R.S.V.P.* meaning *please reply*; and *N.B.* and *PS* both used when you are adding a footnote to a letter. See if you can find out what they actually stand for and the languages they come from.

Exercise 69
Write out the conjunctions in each of the following sentences:
(1) Call in before you go, and don't worry if it's late, as I shall still be up.
(2) Either watch by the door, or, since it will be quite dark by then, go inside; but keep quiet.
(3) Although it was fine we took our macs, as rain had been forecast for the afternoon.

Exercise 70
Put in the correct form of the verb in these sentences.
(1) Both Derek and I are/am/is going to the party.   (2) Jack and Jill is/are going up the hill.
(3) Not only the general, but also the entire regiment has/have been captured.
(4) Not only all the soldiers but also their general has/have surrendered to the enemy.
(5) Neither John nor Mary speak/speaks Urdu.   (6) Either Frederick or I am/are/is going.
(7) Neither of the alternatives is/are acceptable.   (8) Both of the alternatives is/are unacceptable.
(9) Neither of the girls want/wants to come, nor does/do either of the boys.

Exercise 71
Rewrite the following passage, putting in the speech marks (inverted commas), and speech paragraphs where they are required. The rest of the punctuation is already there to assist you.

Hello in there! called Flip. Come on, somebody. Let me in. What's the password ? came the reply. Oh, I don't know. Is it 'Marmalade'? No. Try again! Look, if that's you Andrew, you had better just open this door and let me in, shouted Flip, and gave the planks a kick to emphasize his point. I'm supposed to be Deputy Chief, don't forget, he added, in what he hoped was a menacing tone. I could have you put on trial for insub... insuport.... disobedience. And I could have you put on trial for not knowing the password. That's far worse, replied Andrew. Oh, for goodness sake, let him in, Andrew, interrupted Peter from inside, or I shall put you both on trial for being total idiots. The sound of fumbling with large and rusty bolts came from inside, and Flip pushed his way in past Andrew. He's the idiot, not me, he insisted angrily, giving Andrew a hefty shove. I think I should give him an official punishment for insub... Don't start that again, ordered Peter.

Exercise 72
Change each sentence from direct into indirect speech.
(1) "Have you boys been playing in the coal hole ?" asked Mrs Stevenson angrily.
(2) "I am not going to the match this afternoon," said Christopher.
(3) "Stop it at once !" said their father. "I cannot hear myself think for the noise you are making."
(4) "Do you like that Jane Sopwith ?" Ermintrude asked me. "She's not my friend any more."
(5) "I was getting on with my work until you came in, " sighed father.
(6) "I was wondering if you were joining us on the beach tomorrow," said Alison.
(7) "Are there any vacancies in the hotel," Jack asked the clerk, "or are you full up ?"
(8) "You must hide me!" he cried, catching hold of my coat. "Don't let them find me!"
(9) "Come up and see me some time, " she whispered, and added: "I'm always in."
(10) "We do not know what you want here, and we do not intend to help you get it, " replied Joe.

Exercise 73

In these sentences the subjunctive could be used. Change the appropriate verb to this usage.

(1) If only he was here now.   (2)   If he betrays me, I shall still have triumphed.

(3) May the powers of darkness take him and his vessel forever.

(4) Though he prays for death, death shall never come to him.

(5) I propose that the motion is now put to the house.

Exercise 74

Correct the punctuation of these sentences.

The errors are all connected with full stops, question marks and exclamation marks.

(1) He asked me what I was doing ? I replied that I wasn't doing anything !

(2) "Can you see a light," I asked ? "Yes "! he replied. "I can see a light over there through the fog !"

(3) "You are with us, Cardew," he asked, raising a cynical eyebrow ?

(4) I can nearly reach it. Give me your hand. And I'll try to pull you up. No. Don't drop the rope.

Exercise 75

Correct the punctuation of these sentences. But do not correct a sentence that is already correct...

The errors are all connected with commas: replacing, inserting or removing them.

(1) The man, that I saw, is over there.   (2) The man that I saw, is over there.

(3) The man that I saw is over there I think   (4) Give me a handkerchief please Teddy.

(5) I must have made a mistake, he is however, very like the man for whom the police are searching.

(6) Bring me a box of matches some of those candles, and a length of rope.

(7) Do you want any or not, hurry up, and tell me, I can't wait all day you know.

(8) Nevertheless the sea is visible from the hotel if you have a telescope, and a step-ladder that is.

(9) With a startled cry forgetting the bucket, that he was holding Freddie the youngest of the boys jumped from the ladder and landed amongst the others scattering whitewash in all directions.

(10) The defendant one Bill Sykes is charged with aggravated burglary arson attempted murder and keeping a dog, known as 'Bullseye' and here produced as exhibit A My Lord without a licence.

Exercise 76

Insert in the following sentences: one colon, one semi colon, one dash, one pair of brackets and one pair of quotation marks. All the other punctuation is there, and does not need to be changed.

(1) You will need a milk bottle, a piece of string, four jam-jar lids, two skewers and some gunpowder.

(2) We can choose Bill if you really want to I'm still not sure he's the right man for the job, though.

(3) "Just wait for me in the outer office third door on the right," said Jackson.

(4) Have you read Gray's Elegy in a Country Churchyard, my boy ?

(5) There is no doubt with all due deference to the opposition that this measure is necessary.

Exercise 77

Find out what the following abbreviations mean, and give their full forms:

(1) UNESCO   (2) L.B.W.   (3) SSE   (4) C.O.   (5) U.K.   (6) P.O.   (7) P.T.

(8) c.o.d.   (9) lat.   (10) mm   (11) BSc   (12) pp   (13) o.n.o.   (14) Lt.

(15) NB   (16) Q.E.D.   (17) op cit.   (18) p.m.   (19) p.a.   (20) R.S.V.P.

INDEX OF MAIN TOPICS
Listed Alphabetically with Rule Numbers

Not every mention of every topic is listed, only those where the most important information will be found. Where several rules are quoted, it is advisable to check the first mention first, as this will often give a definition or basic explanation of the topic concerned.